BOLD & BOSSY

UNLEASHING THE POWER OF WOMEN IN BUSINESS

WOMEN'S GUIDE TO BUSINESS BRILLANCE

BUILDING
SCALING
SUCCEEDING

MOLLY STEWART

Bold and Bossy: Women's Guide to Business Brilliance

" Unleashing the Power of Women in Business"

Building, Scaling, Succeeding

Written by Molly Stewart

Table of Content

Contents

INTRODUCTION

Welcome to "Bold and Bossy: Women's Guide to Business Brilliance – Unleashing the Power of Women in Business." In the dynamic landscape of entrepreneurship, the indomitable spirit of women has been a driving force for innovation, resilience, and success.

In the pages that follow, we embark on a transformative journey that goes beyond conventional business wisdom. "Bold and Bossy" is not just a guide; it's a manifesto for women who dare to dream big, disrupt industries, and redefine success on their own terms. This book is a call to action for every woman who aspires to leave an indelible mark in the business world.

The dynamic world of entrepreneurial exploration with " Bold and Bossy: Women's Guide to Business Brilliance: Navigating the Path to Business Brilliance." In the ever-evolving landscape of business, where innovation meets tenacity, this book serves as a compass for aspiring entrepreneurs and seasoned visionaries alike.

Whether you're embarking on your maiden entrepreneurial voyage or seeking to elevate your existing ventures, the pages that unfold will be a source of inspiration, guidance, and strategic insight.

" Bold and Bossy: Women's Guide to Business Brilliance " is more than a guide; it's a roadmap for those who dare to dream big, challenge the status quo, and bring their unique visions to life. As we traverse the exhilarating terrain of entrepreneurship, we'll delve into the essential principles, unconventional strategies, and real-world anecdotes that define the journey from concept to success.

This book is a celebration of the entrepreneurial spirit, where creativity meets resilience, and where every setback becomes a stepping stone to greater achievements. We'll explore the stories of trailblazers who have transformed industries, disrupted norms, and forged their own paths to brilliance.

From crafting a compelling business strategy to mastering the art of effective leadership, from navigating the complexities of funding to harnessing the power of adaptability – " Bold and Bossy: Women's Guide to Business Brilliance " equips you with the tools to not only survive but thrive in the competitive landscape of entrepreneurship.

Whether you're a budding entrepreneur or a seasoned business maven, prepare to be challenged, inspired, and empowered to embrace the exhilarating journey of bringing your venture vision to fruition. " Bold and Bossy: Women's Guide to Business Brilliance " is your companion on the quest for entrepreneurial excellence – where innovation, strategy, and passion converge to create lasting impact.

The adventure begins now. Welcome to a world where your entrepreneurial vision becomes a reality.

We delve into the unique challenges faced by women in business and provide empowering insights, strategies, and real-life stories that inspire and guide. From conquering self-doubt to mastering negotiation, from building thriving networks to leveraging the power of mentorship – "Bold and Bossy" equips you with the tools to navigate the entrepreneurial landscape with confidence and brilliance.

The business world is evolving, and women are at the forefront of this evolution. It's time to embrace your boldness, own your brilliance, and become the boss you were born to be. "Bold and Bossy" is more than a book; it's a movement, a community of fearless women supporting each other as they rise to the pinnacle of success.

Get ready to unleash your power, break through barriers, and make your mark. The journey to business brilliance starts now. Welcome to "Bold and Bossy."

Chapter 1

Finding Your Passion and Purpose

Finding your passion and purpose is the first crucial step in the thrilling journey of entrepreneurship that will lead to success and fulfilment.

This chapter acts as a compass, assisting you in discovering your true motivations and sources of inspiration through introspection.

Recognizing Your Passions

- Think about the things that get you excited to start.
- Recall times when you were so focused on something that time just seemed to fly.
- Enumerate the hobbies and pursuits that bring your personal fulfilments.

Determining What You Enjoy Doing

- Think about the emotional component of your passions.
- What activities makes you happy, content, and proud of yourself?
- Pay attention to how different activities make you feel; this can reveal insights into your true passions.

Identifying Trends in Your Enthusiastic Activities

- As you reflect on them, look for recurring themes or threads that relate your interests. Whether it is a passion for creativity or figuring out problems.

Examining Potential Markets

- Examining Market Trends and Industries.
- Turn your attention to the surrounding environment.
- Look into new market trends and different industries.

This investigation will help you connect your passion with possible business growth areas while also broadening your perspective.

Evaluating Opportunities and Demand in Different Sectors

- Analyse the needs of the market and find prospects that would suit your interests.

- Often, addressing unfulfilled needs or resolving issues within an industry leads to a successful venture.

Matching Your Interest to Industry Demands

- Make sure the venture you're pursuing not only aligns with your passion but also addresses legitimate market needs.
- Finding a balance between practicality and personal fulfilments is the foundation of a sustainable business model.

Evaluating Your Capabilities and Advantages

- Assess your soft and hard skill sets.
- What skills come naturally to you?

To create a business that plays to your strengths, it is essential to understand your skill set.

Identifying Transferable Competencies

- Ascertain the skills you possess from prior experiences that you can utilize in your entrepreneurial endeavours.
- A unique skill set that is appropriate for your organization can often be created by combining talents from different roles.

Making the Most of Your Special Skills in Business

- Make a strategy that capitalizes on your unique advantages. Whether you have a keen sense of detail or exceptional communication skills, using these advantages in your business plan will set you apart from the competition.

Outlining Your Principles

- Determining Your Personal and Professional Core Values.
- Explore your values, or the tenets that steer your choices.
- Examine the principles that are important to you personally and think about how your company can be built around them.

Making Sure Your Business Choices Comply with Your Values

- Make the choice to conduct your company morally and in accordance with your basic beliefs. Gaining the trust of your stakeholders can be achieved by being sincere and incorporating your values into your business processes.

Establishing a Business That Upholds Your Moral Principles

- Be open and honest about your ethical standards.
- Long-term business success is facilitated by aligning your enterprise with ethical standards, be it social responsibility or environmental sustainability.

Setting Goals and Objectives

- Establishing Short-Term and Long-Term Goals.
- Define your goals, both short-term and long-term. Short-term goals provide immediate direction, while long-term goals create a vision for the future trajectory of your business.

- **Creating SMART Objectives**

Make sure your objectives are SMART.: Specific, Measurable, Achievable, Relevant, and Time-bound. This framework improves understanding and offers a guide for tracking advancement.

- **Organizing Your Business Goals**

Create a graphic business plan that shows the direction your company is going. This map is a flexible tool that changes with your entrepreneurial journey.

- **Crafting a Vision Statement That Is Powerful**

Write a brief vision statement that captures the essence of your entrepreneurial experience. A strong vision statement motivates those around you and acts as a road map for your activities.

• Connecting Your Vision to Your Passion and Purpose

- Verify that your vision, passion, and purpose are all perfectly aligned.

 This alignment provides the foundation for a successful and incredibly fulfilling business.

Crafting Your Entrepreneurial Vision

- Thinking Ahead for Your Company's Future
- Consider your company's future.
- Imagine the difference and the legacy you hope to leave behind.

 This creative exercise sharpens your focus and determines the course of your endeavours.

Chapter 2

Passion and Determination

Developing passion and tenacity are essential for long-term business success. Passion is the driving force behind an entrepreneurial mindset, and entrepreneurs are driven by an intense excitement for their concepts, endeavours, and objectives. Your enthusiasm for your work gives you the perseverance and determination to overcome the difficulties that come with being an entrepreneur.

Entrepreneurs are propelled forward by a fierce desire for success despite obstacles, disappointments, and the inevitable highs and lows of the entrepreneurial journey. In addition to an unwavering commitment to goal achievement, the combination of these two inherently entrepreneurial dynamic forces results in resilience, inventiveness, and goal-pursuing energy.

Never forget that willpower and passion need to be actively developed; they are not fixed. Maintaining the entrepreneurial spirit requires you to evaluate your progress, stay focused on your objectives, and surround yourself with supportive people.

Here are some strategies to help you develop and maintain these qualities:

1. Determine your motivation.
- Clearly state your objectives and the rationale behind launching your own company.
- Having a clear vision for the impact you want to make will keep you motivated when times are difficult.
2. Make intentional goals.
- Establish realistic short- and long-term goals that advance your vision.
- Set realistic short- and long-term objectives that help you realize your vision. To preserve a sense of progress, break down more ambitious objectives into smaller, more manageable tasks.
3. Determine which market segment actually excites and piques your interest by finding your enthusiastic specialization.

- Maintaining motivation when working on a project you are passionate about and strongly believe in is common.

4. Maintain an optimistic outlook
- Adopt an optimistic mindset and concentrate on finding solutions rather than problems.
- Make sure you are in the company of people, things, or reading that will encourage you.

5. Agree to take risks
- Rather than viewing challenges as obstacles, view them as chances for personal growth.
- Overcoming challenges can help you become more resolute and passionate.

6. Continuous Learning:
- Stay curious and committed to learning in your field.
- Gaining new knowledge and skills can rekindle your passion and keep you at the forefront of your industry.

7. Establish an Aid Network/ Create a support system
- Establish a network of mentors, business associates, and like-minded people.
- Learn from others, impart your experiences, and ask for guidance.

8. Honour Minor Victories/ Celebrate small wins
- No matter how small, acknowledge and celebrate your successes.
- Progress is a motivator and source of excitement.

9. Visualize Your Achievement: Make a clear picture of what you've done.
- Visualization helps fortify your resolve and keep you concentrated on your goal.

The Fire of Passion

The spark that starts an entrepreneurial endeavour is passion. This company owner is passionate about their endeavors, ideas, or causes. This passion is more than just a hobby; it's a powerful drive that provides the perseverance and fortitude required to achieve long-term goals

1. Intrinsic Motivation:

Passion is an internal motivator that remains unaffected by advantages from outside sources. This kind of thinking inspires business owners who genuinely love what they do and have goals beyond financial gain. They have an intrinsic motivation that allows them to persevere through challenges and keep their perspective.

2. Converting Obstacles into Possibilities

Transforming obstacles into opportunities rather than seeing insurmountable obstacles, driven entrepreneurs see opportunities for growth and innovation. Those who have an entrepreneurial mindset concentrate on coming up with creative solutions, taking lessons from past errors, and using adversity as a launching pad for success when faced with challenges.

3. The ability to bounce back from setbacks

Entrepreneurship is a difficult journey with many obstacles along the way, but passion is a constant motivator. Entrepreneurs overcome obstacles with a strong sense of passion and determination. Rather, they turn obstacles into teaching moments, exhibiting a resolute will to endure and gain knowledge from every experience.

4. Determination to Achieve Goals

Entrepreneurs are determined to achieve their goals with tenacity and determination. Persistent entrepreneurs, who bear down in the face of setbacks, disappointments, and uncertain times, display this kind of thinking. People are inspired to keep going forward by this perseverance, even in the face of hardship.

5. Motivating and Inspiring Teams

Entrepreneurs who are passionate and driven inspire others. Their infectious energy inspires teammates, partners, and stakeholders to share their vision. This ability to inspire fosters a constructive and cooperative environment, bolstering the group's effort to achieve shared objectives.

6. **Personal Growth Commitment**

Business owners who are passionate and tenacious recognize the link between personal development and business success. They are dedicated to improving their skills, learning new things, and bettering themselves. Their dedication to personal development ensures that they can remain adaptable and creative in an ever-changing business environment.

7. **Managing Ambition and Realism**

Ambition is fuelled by passion, but determination ensures a balanced approach. This type of entrepreneur strikes a delicate balance between lofty ambitions and execution realities. Because of this practical approach that promotes long-term progress, they can set motivating and attainable goals.

8. **Cultivating Passion and Determination**

As we explore the entrepreneurial mindset, we'll look at doable strategies in this section for inspiring passion and tenacity in both your team and yourself. By embracing these characteristics, you not only give your entrepreneurial endeavours purpose, but you also establish the foundation for long-term success.

Consider how your passion and perseverance can transform the way you approach opportunities and obstacles, serving as guiding lights in your pursuit of entrepreneurial greatness.

9. **Adaptability and Flexibility**

An entrepreneur thinks in a fluid and adaptive way. Entrepreneurs are aware of changes in consumer preferences, markets, and technological advancements. A crucial aspect of the entrepreneurial mindset is the capacity to quickly adapt to these changes.

In addition to being desirable traits in the dynamic world of entrepreneurship, adaptability and flexibility are fundamental elements of the entrepreneurial mindset. In the quick-changing world of innovation and business, entrepreneurs who welcome change, deal with uncertainty, and adjust fast to new circumstances not only survive but prosper.

We'll examine the mindset of an entrepreneur and discuss strategies for enhancing and growing flexibility and adaptability. By adopting these traits, you can help your group or company create a resilient and creative culture and put yourself in a position to successfully negotiate the difficulties of entrepreneurship.

Think about how being flexible can help you revaluate and react to opportunities and challenges, which will improve your agility and responsiveness in a dynamic work environment.

10. Recognizing Change as a Constant

The first step toward becoming adaptable is accepting that change is an inevitable and ongoing part of being an entrepreneur. This way of thinking allows entrepreneurs to see change as an opportunity for growth and advancement rather than a hindrance. They recognize that in a world where market dynamics are constantly changing, flexibility is a tactical advantage.

11. Proactive Market Trend Response

Entrepreneurs who are adaptable, closely monitor market trends and act quickly to address any changes that may occur. Adaptable people can anticipate trends and adjust their strategies accordingly, whether they are related to industry norms, developments in technology or shifts in customer tastes. They are able to keep one step ahead of the competition as a result.

12. Adaptability in Making Decisions

Flexibility in decision-making is necessary to change course and strategy. Adaptive entrepreneurs take a variety of factors into account when making decisions, such as market feedback, data analytics, and changing circumstances. Their adaptability enables them to react quickly to fresh knowledge and evolving circumstances.

13. **Quickness in problem-solving**:

Agile problem-solving and adaptability are closely related ideas. This type of thinking allows entrepreneurs to follow pre-set solutions with flexibility. Rather, they have an open mind when it comes to problems and are willing to explore unusual and innovative solutions. They can overcome unforeseen obstacles with resilience and creativity thanks to their agility.

14. **Adaptable entrepreneurs cultivate**

- **Fast Reaction to Opportunities**: In a fast-paced business setting, unforeseen opportunities can arise. Adaptable entrepreneurs are quick to recognize and take advantage of these opportunities. They can quickly change course and gain a competitive advantage because of their ability to align resources with emerging opportunities.

The ability to be flexible is a crucial trait for managing the uncertainty that accompanies being an entrepreneur. Entrepreneurs can take on uncertainty head-on and leverage it to generate creative ideas and strategic research by adopting this way of thinking. They know that adaptability is a strength and are at ease working in unclear circumstances.

15. **Integrating adaptability into culture**

Not only is adaptation a personal trait, but it can also be fostered as a cultural trait within a group or company. Change-friendly, education-focused, and team-sharing-oriented cultures are fostered by flexible entrepreneurs. Innovation and resilience are encouraged by this cultural integration.

16. **Continuous Learning and Skill Development**

Being adaptable requires a dedication to lifelong learning and skill improvement. Entrepreneurs that have this mentality understand that continuing education is necessary to remain relevant in a world that is changing quickly. They make an investment in learning new skills and support their teams in doing the same, which guarantees a flexible and dynamic workforce.

Innovative Thinking

The core of entrepreneurship is innovation. So, we can say Innovation is the lifeblood of entrepreneurship. An entrepreneurial mindset is characterized by a dedication to original thought, questioning the status quo, and continuously looking for new and improved ways to provide value.

We'll look at practical strategies for cultivating and enhancing innovative thinking as we investigate the entrepreneurial mindset. Adopting these principles not only positions you as a forward-thinking entrepreneur, but it also fosters a culture of continuous innovation within your team or organization. Consider how innovative thinking can reframe your approach to problems and opportunities, propelling your ventures into uncharted territory.

Entrepreneurs aim to create something novel and significant because they are dissatisfied with the status quo.

The ability to think creatively is a fundamental component of the entrepreneurial mindset.

Innovative entrepreneurs constantly push the envelope of what is feasible, question the status quo, and look for fresh approaches to problems.

1. Challenging Conventional Wisdom

Creative thinkers are not constrained by received wisdom. They scrutinize established conventions, contest customary methods, and explore substitutes that may result in more effective or significant results. Through questioning the current state of affairs, entrepreneurs make space for innovative concepts and game-changing fixes.

2. Cultivating a Creative Mindset

A creative mindset is the foundation of innovative thinking. This type of entrepreneur approaches problems creatively and curiously. They see obstacles as chances to let their creativity flow, trying out novel concepts and unorthodox methods. Creating an atmosphere that values and promotes creativity is a key component of developing a creative mindset.

3. Cross-Disciplinary Collaboration

Innovation frequently thrives at the crossroads of different disciplines. Entrepreneurs who think creatively, actively seek cross-disciplinary collaboration, bringing together people with different skills and perspectives. The interaction of various disciplines creates a rich ecosystem of ideas and solutions.

4. Encouraging Idea Generation

Innovative thinkers actively encourage team members to generate ideas. They create environments conducive to brainstorming, ideation sessions, and open dialogue. This inclusive approach not only generates a diverse range of perspectives, but also empowers team members to contribute their unique insights, fostering an innovative culture.

5. Experimentation and Risk-Taking

Experimentation and risk-taking are required for innovation. Entrepreneurs who think creatively are willing to try new approaches, test hypotheses, and accept failure as a stepping stone to success. This experimental mindset fosters a culture in which calculated risks are viewed as necessary for progress.

6. User-Centric Design

Innovative entrepreneurs prioritize user-centric design, ensuring that products or solutions are tailored to meet the needs and preferences of their target audience. By understanding the user experience and incorporating feedback, they create solutions that resonate with their customers, setting the stage for market success.

7. Adopting Technology and Trends

Innovation often involves leveraging emerging technologies and staying abreast of industry trends. Entrepreneurs with innovative thinking actively adopt and adapt to technological advancements, positioning their ventures at the forefront of industry evolution. They recognize the transformative potential of technology in enhancing products, processes, and customer experiences.

8. Learning from Failure and Iteration

Innovation is considered an iterative process where learning from mistakes is considered beneficial. Innovative businesspeople examine their mistakes, draw lessons from them, and apply these revelations to hone and enhance their concepts. This ability to bounce back from setbacks adds to the continuous cycle of innovation.

9. Fostering a Culture of Innovation

Not only is innovative thinking a personal talent, but it's also a team or organizational culture that can be fostered. Innovative entrepreneurs cultivate an environment that honours and incentivizes creative thought. They foster an atmosphere where team members are encouraged to share ideas and take measured chances.

<u>Resourcefulness</u>

Entrepreneurs excel at making the most of the resources at their disposal. When faced with constraints, the entrepreneurial mindset is resourceful, finding creative and efficient ways to achieve goals. This resourcefulness is a key driver of entrepreneurial success.

The ability to navigate challenges creatively and effectively, leveraging available resources to achieve goals, is a cornerstone of the entrepreneurial mindset. Entrepreneurs with a resourceful mindset excel at coming up with novel solutions, adapting to constraints, and turning challenges into opportunities.

In this section, we'll look at the principles and strategies for developing resourcefulness.

1. **Creative Problem-Solving**
   - Entrepreneurs with a creative mindset approach problems.
   - They see challenges as opportunities to demonstrate their ingenuity rather than as insurmountable obstacles.
   - Thinking outside the box, exploring unconventional solutions, and adapting strategies to fit the unique circumstances of a situation are all part of creative problem-solving.

2. **Optimizing Existing Resources**
   - Prior to seeking additional resources, resourcefulness entails optimizing existing ones.
   - Entrepreneurs with this mindset evaluate their tools, talents, and assets to maximize their utility.
   - This optimization not only improves efficiency, but it also fosters a mindset of making the most of what is available.

3. **Leveraging Networks and Relationships**
   - Entrepreneurs understand the value of networks and relationships as resources.

- Utilizing connections with mentors, peers, and industry experts is part of having a resourceful mindset.
- Entrepreneurs gain access to knowledge, advice, and potential collaborations by tapping into a variety of networks.

4. Efficient Time Management

Time is a valuable resource, and resourceful entrepreneurs are masters of time management. They prioritize tasks, establish clear goals, and avoid distractions. Effective time management allows entrepreneurs to focus on high-impact activities while increasing productivity and meeting goals on time.

5. Financial Resourcefulness

Financial limitations are a common occurrence in entrepreneurship, and astute business people know how to deal with them.

This entails creating a sensible budget, looking for economical fixes, and investigating different funding sources. Financial resourcefulness makes sure that businesses can weather economic downturns and continue to operate.

6. Adapting to Constraints

The capacity to adjust to limitations is a sign of resourcefulness. This kind of entrepreneur sees constraints as opportunities for innovation rather than as obstacles to overcome.

Finding innovative solutions to accomplish objectives in the face of resource shortages—such as those related to time, money, or labour—represents adapting to constraints.

7. Learning from Setbacks

Resourceful entrepreneurs use setbacks as stepping stones for future success. Rather than moping around mistakes, they look into the root causes, glean important lessons, and apply these understandings to future strategies.

This never-ending process of learning supports an entrepreneurial path that is robust and expanding.

8. Adopting Tools and Technology

Strategic use of technology by astute entrepreneurs can make it a powerful tool. They employ technology to boost productivity, mechanize workflows, and maintain their competitiveness in a quickly evolving digital environment. One of the most crucial aspects of resourcefulness is embracing and modifying new technologies.

9. Scalability and Sustainability

The ability to be resourceful extends to the scalability and sustainability of ventures. Entrepreneurs with this mindset plan for growth by creating scalable processes and ensuring that the business model can adapt to increased demand.

This forward-thinking approach contributes to long-term sustainability and success.

Cultivating a Culture of Resourcefulness

Resourcefulness is a cultural trait that can be fostered within a team or organization, not just an individual trait. Entrepreneurs with resourceful mindset foster a culture that values creativity, problem-solving, and resource efficiency. This resourcefulness culture encourages team members to contribute ideas and solutions.

We'll look at practical strategies for cultivating and enhancing resourcefulness as we investigate the entrepreneurial mindset. By adopting these principles, you not only position yourself as a resourceful entrepreneur, but you also foster an innovation and efficiency culture within your team or organization. Consider how resourcefulness can change the way you approach challenges and opportunities, opening up new paths to success.

1. A Long-Term Perspective

The entrepreneurial mindset is focused on long-term success, even though short-term objectives and benchmarks are frequently included in entrepreneurial endeavours. When making decisions, entrepreneurs use a strategic mindset, taking long-term viability and scalability into account.

Adopting these core values is necessary to comprehend the entrepreneurial mindset.

An essential component of the entrepreneurial mindset is a long-term view, which includes the capacity to envision and strive for long-term, sustainable success. This type of entrepreneur looks past quick profits and concentrates on creating long-lasting businesses and making choices that extend the life of their projects. We'll look at the ideas and methods for developing a long-term perspective in this section.

2. Strategic Planning for Sustainable Growth

Planning strategically with sustainable growth as a top priority is essential to a long-term outlook. This kind of thinking helps entrepreneurs establish attainable long-term goals and create plans of action that support them. By using a strategic approach, all decisions are made with the long-term vision and success of the venture in mind.

3. Building Strong Foundations

Establishing strong foundations for their companies is the focus of entrepreneurs. This means investing time and energy into developing a culture that fosters long-term success, solidifying operational procedures, and organizing the company. Establishing a solid base offers resilience and stability, both of which are critical for navigating obstacles and unpredictability.

4. Customer-Centric Value Proposition

Creating and providing value for customers is at the core of a long-term outlook. This kind of entrepreneur places a high value on knowing their customers, forming trusting bonds with them, and continuously changing their products to satisfy changing needs. A customer-focused strategy helps ensure long-term success and brand loyalty.

5. Investing in Human Capital

Long-term-focused business owners understand the value of making human capital investments. This entails developing a positive work environment, hiring and keeping talented people, and offering opportunities for professional growth. Any venture's long-term success depends on developing a talented and driven team.

6. Risk Management and Contingency Planning

A strategic approach to risk management is necessary for long-term success. Long-term-oriented entrepreneurs conduct thorough risk analyses and create backup strategies. Proactive risk management guarantees the venture's ability to overcome unforeseen obstacles and maintain its resilience over time.

7. Adapting to Market Trends

Market dynamics change, and a long-term perspective requires adapting to these changes. Entrepreneurs are constantly on the lookout for market trends, emerging technologies, and shifts in consumer behaviour.

By staying on top of these changes, they can proactively adjust strategies to stay relevant and seize new opportunities for long-term growth.

8. Environmental and Social Responsibility

Sustainability encompasses social and environmental responsibility in addition to financial success. Long-term-oriented entrepreneurs incorporate sustainable practices into their business operations, taking into account the effects of their endeavours on society and the environment. This dedication to accountability is in line with changing social norms.

9. Strategic Alliances and Partnerships

Creating a long-term perspective requires strategic planning, adaptability, and a commitment to long-term success.

Long-term success is largely dependent on collaboration. This kind of thinking drives entrepreneurs to look for strategic partnerships and alliances that will expand their capabilities and foster mutual growth.

Developing trusting bonds with stakeholders and other companies broadens the network and opens doors for long-term success.

Having a long-term perspective necessitates investing in innovation for future relevance. Entrepreneurs are constantly looking for fresh and creative ways to enhance their products, services, and workflows in order to stay ahead of the competition. This proactive approach ensures that initiatives remain relevant in a rapidly evolving business environment.

10. Success Is Determined by Factors Other Than Cash

While financial metrics remain important, assessing long-term success goes beyond monetary gains. Entrepreneurs take into account a variety of factors, including the satisfaction of their customers, employee engagement, and social impact. A thorough plan for success is in line with the company's long-term objectives.

Your Role in the Entrepreneurial Journey

Think about how you fit into the entrepreneurial journey as you turn the pages ahead of you. This inquiry is meant to empower and direct you, regardless of whether you're an innovator prepared to start a business or someone trying to incorporate entrepreneurial thinking into your ongoing projects.

Understanding the Entrepreneurial Mindset:

It's critical to understand that the entrepreneurial mindset is a way of thinking and approaching the world rather than just a collection of abilities. Visionaries are entrepreneurs; they see opportunities where others see obstacles. Their journey towards achieving their dreams is fuelled by a special blend of ambition, creativity, and resilience that they possess.

The key to success for anyone stepping into the fast-paced, frequently unpredictable realm of entrepreneurship is having an entrepreneurial mindset. It encompasses a distinct combination of mindset, convictions, and methods of thinking that set entrepreneurs apart from others.

We will examine the essential elements of the entrepreneurial mindset in this section, providing insight into what makes it such a potent force in the business world.

1. Vision and Opportunity Recognition

Seeing opportunities where others see obstacles is the fundamental trait of an entrepreneurial mindset. Rich businesspeople can identify market opportunities and anticipate trends ahead of time because they have excellent vision. It is this progressive mentality that drives business growth and innovation.

2. Risk-Taking and Decision-Making

Entrepreneurs acknowledge that a necessary component of the process is taking calculated risks. They understand that striving for success will always entail some risk. The characteristics of an entrepreneurial mindset include the capacity to make decisions in the face of uncertainty and the resilience to overcome both successes and setbacks.

3. Innovation and Creativity

Creativity feeds the spirit of enterprise. Entrepreneurs think outside the box to find creative solutions to problems and to challenge the status quo. This kind of thinking encourages a never-ending quest of perfection and the willingness to question the status quo in order to create something novel and valuable.

4. Adaptability and Resilience

The world of entrepreneurship is always changing. Entrepreneurs are highly adaptive individuals who modify their tactics and approaches in reaction to changing conditions. Entrepreneurs can overcome obstacles with persistence when they possess resilience, or the capacity to overcome setbacks.

5. Resourcefulness and Problem-Solving

Entrepreneurs are ingenious people who thrive at solving challenging issues. The entrepreneurial mindset entails taking the initiative to get past roadblocks, making innovative use of the resources at hand, and transforming setbacks into learning experiences.

6. Passion and Commitment

The motivation behind many prosperous business endeavour's is passion. The mentality entails a strong dedication to one's vision and objectives, providing the perseverance required to overcome challenges. Enthusiastic businesspeople uplift others and have a beneficial effect on their groups and societies.

7. Long-Term Vision and Goal Orientation:

Entrepreneurs consider long-term objectives and sustainable success rather than just short-term profits. The mentality entails goal-setting, strategic planning, and the capacity to endure the unavoidable highs and lows of the entrepreneurial path.

Chapter 3

The Entrepreneurial Mindset & Developing a Winning Mindset

Establishing a business requires more than just a well-written business plan; it also necessitates a resilient and imaginative mindset. In this chapter, we dive into the psychological aspects of entrepreneurship and examine the fundamentals of a winning mindset.

Introduction to the Entrepreneurial Mindset

Welcome to the dynamic world of entrepreneurship, where individuals can achieve success not only through financial planning and business acumen, but also by adopting a mindset that helps them seize opportunities, get past challenges, and thrive in the dynamic environment of invention and creation.

Entrepreneurial mindsets form the foundation of successful ventures. It explores the beliefs, attitudes, and points of view that set entrepreneurs apart and goes beyond conventional business knowledge.

In this chapter, we'll delve deeply into the foundations of the entrepreneurial mindset and discover how it affects the path to happiness and prosperity.

The Entrepreneurial Mindset: Definition:

Fundamentally, the entrepreneurial mindset is a collection of attitudes and convictions that inspire people to envision, create, and overcome obstacles in the business world. It's an innovative method of approaching problem-solving and seizing opportunities that goes above and beyond standard business procedures.

Comprehending this mentality is essential not only for initiating and expanding a prosperous enterprise but also for nurturing a mindset that promotes individual development and satisfaction.

The entrepreneurial mindset is an approach to problem-solving and an orientation towards opportunity that goes beyond a simple skill set.

We'll go deeper into useful techniques for developing and putting visionary thinking into practice during this examination of the entrepreneurial mindset, giving you the ability to picture a world full of opportunities. As we go along, think about how adopting a visionary mindset can change the way you approach opportunities and challenges and lead you to a future where your only limitations are your imagination.

1. Visionary Thinking (Creative Thought)

The foundation of entrepreneurial thinking is the capacity to look beyond the here and now and imagine a future that others may not yet be able to see. Entrepreneurs are visionaries who are always looking around them for new opportunities, market gaps, and creative solutions.

One of the main components of the entrepreneurial mindset in the field of entrepreneurship is visionary thinking. It encompasses the capacity to see beyond the here and now, to imagine opportunities that others might miss, and to map out a path toward an exciting and meaningful future.

For those who want to succeed in the ever-changing world of innovation and creation, it is imperative that they comprehend and practice visionary thinking.

- **Seeing Beyond the Immediate (Looking Past the Here and Now)**

Having the ability to look beyond the present situation is the first step towards visionary thinking. This kind of thinking gives entrepreneurs a special perspective that lets them look ahead and predict trends, changes in technology, and new business opportunities.

Visionary thinkers put themselves in a position to profit from the next big idea by seeing beyond the status quo.

- **Seeing the Possibilities**

Visionary thinking is essentially the ability to see opportunities where others might see obstacles. This kind of thinking gives entrepreneurs the natural ability to spot market gaps, predict customer needs, and come up with creative solutions.

They are able to establish themselves as innovators in their fields thanks to this progressive mindset.

- **Visualizing the Unvisible**

Thinkers with vision are skilled at seeing possibilities that are not yet apparent. They disprove accepted beliefs, stretch the bounds of imagination, and create an atmosphere that is conducive to the growth of innovative ideas. This creative ability is not constrained by the constraints of the present; rather, it is fed by the conviction that the seemingly unattainable can come to pass.

- **Setting a Compelling Direction (Determining an Intriguing Path)**

Beyond just fantasy, visionary thinking entails establishing a compelling course for the future. These kind of entrepreneurs not only have lofty dreams, but they also lay out a plan for converting their ideas into real, attainable objectives. Their pursuit of long-term success is energized by this distinct sense of direction, which directs their strategic decision-making.

- **Embracing Change as an Opportunity / Accepting Change as a Possibility**

Change is seen as an opportunity rather than a threat by visionary thinkers. They recognize that as technology advances, so do industries and consumer preferences. Visionary thinkers welcome change, putting themselves in a position to quickly adjust and profit from new trends rather than fighting it.

- **Motivating Other People**

The capacity to motivate and inspire others toward a common goal is a fundamental component of visionary thinking. Entrepreneurs who possess this mentality inspire a group of people or a community by passionately and firmly communicating their ideas. Gaining support and converting a vision into a group mission are made possible by this inspirational leadership.

- **Keeping Aspiration and Realism in Check**

Though bold aspirations are encouraged by visionary thinking, a certain amount of realism is also necessary. Ambitious vision and realistic execution are balanced by successful entrepreneurs. They establish a vision that is both attainable and motivating, setting the stage for long-term growth and success.

- **Cultivating Visionary Thinking/ Developing a Forward-Looking Perspective**

A compelling vision must be communicated, creativity must be nurtured, and anticipation must be mastered in order to cultivate visionary thinking.

2. Proactive Problem-Solving

Problem-solving is an entrepreneurial passion. Rather than considering challenges as impediments, they perceive them as chances for development and enhancement.

The proactive approach to problem-solving that underpins the entrepreneurial mindset involves meeting obstacles head-on with inventiveness and a resolve to come up with workable solutions.

At the core of the entrepreneurial mindset is proactive problem-solving, which demonstrates the capacity to foresee difficulties, deal with them before they become more serious, and turn roadblocks into chances for advancement. Instead of being reactive, this proactive approach gives people the power to actively control their circumstances and skilfully negotiate the challenges of entrepreneurship.

Building a Culture of Proactive Problem-Solving

We will discuss proactive problem-solving techniques that you can implement in your team and organization as we examine the entrepreneurial mindset. Adopting this strategy helps you not only overcome obstacles more skilfully but also foster an innovative and resilient culture that advances your entrepreneurial endeavours.

- **Anticipating Challenges**

Anticipating problems before they arise is the first step towards proactive problem solving. This kind of thinking helps entrepreneurs become acutely aware of any potential roadblocks, such as shifts in the market, problems in their operations, or unanticipated outside influences.

They put themselves in a position to react quickly and strategically by foreseeing obstacles.

- **Strategic Planning**

Strategic planning is the cornerstone of proactive problem-solving. Entrepreneurs develop all-encompassing plans that take into consideration possible future obstacles in addition to present demands. This proactive planning entails defining milestones, creating backup plans to reduce risks, and setting specific goals.

- **Pre-emptive Action/ Preventive Measures**

Proactive problem solvers take preventative measures rather than waiting for problems to get worse. People with this mindset actively look for ways to increase productivity and stop issues from becoming significant roadblocks, whether it's through technology investment, workflow optimization, or business process adjustments.

- **Learning from Failure**

Setbacks are an inevitable part of the entrepreneurial journey, but proactive problem solvers view failure as an invaluable learning opportunity. Rather than moping over errors, they dissect failures to find patterns, comprehend underlying causes, and draw lessons that can guide future tactics. This introspective method encourages ongoing development.

- **Creative Solutions**

Proactive problem-solving aims to generate both creative and problem-solving solutions. This kind of thinking is common among entrepreneurs who approach problems creatively, searching for original and practical answers. They know that often the best responses are the ones that go against what is expected of them.

- **Adjusting to Modifications**

In the ever-changing world of entrepreneurship, change is inevitable. Initiative problem solvers embrace change and proactively adjust their plans to account for evolving circumstances. They remain ahead of the curve by remaining adaptive and flexible in the face of shifting consumer preferences, market trends, or advancements in technology.

- **Effective Communication**

A proactive approach to problem-solving must include communication. Owners who adopt this mentality make sure that lines of communication are clear and open among their employees. They support an environment in which team members are empowered to voice concerns, exchange ideas, and cooperate to find answers.

- **Continuous Improvement**

The attitude of continuous improvement underpins proactive problem-solving. Entrepreneurs evaluate their procedures on a regular basis, look for input, and pinpoint areas that could be improved. Their endeavours stay flexible, effective, and resilient in the face of shifting conditions thanks to their dedication to continuous improvement.

3. Creating a Culture of Adaptability

In this examination of the entrepreneurial mindset, we'll look at methods for building a culture in your team or organization where people feel comfortable facing uncertainty. By fostering this kind of thinking, you may foster an atmosphere that fosters resilience and creativity in addition to improving your ability to navigate the unknown. Proceeding, contemplate how accepting uncertainty might transform your perspective on obstacles and prospects, setting you up for triumph in the capricious path of entrepreneurs

- **Comfort with Uncertainty**

Being an entrepreneur comes with inherent uncertainty, which the entrepreneurial mindset welcomes. Entrepreneurs are at ease in situations where results are uncertain, showing that they are prepared to take measured risks and grow from both achievements and setbacks.

The ability to navigate the dynamic world of entrepreneurship with poise and adaptability is embodied by having an entrepreneurial mindset that is comfortable with uncertainty. Uncertainty presents opportunities for growth, innovation, and success to entrepreneurs who welcome it rather than view it as a barrier.

- **Embracing the Unknown**

People who are at ease with uncertainty don't run from the unknown; rather, they welcome it. They are aware of the uncertainty and ambiguity that often accompany the entrepreneurial path. They take solace in the process of discovery and the possibility of finding new opportunities rather than searching for total certainty.

- **Risk-Taking and Decision-Making**

Risk is a necessary component of innovation and growth, as recognized by entrepreneurs who are at ease with uncertainty. They know that not every decision will turn out as planned when they make it. They are able to make audacious choices that have the potential to yield large rewards because of their willingness to take measured risks.

- **Flexibility and Adaptability**

These traits are frequently required when faced with uncertainty. This type of entrepreneur approaches problems with an open mind, prepared to change course when needed.

They see unforeseen developments as opportunities to revaluate, modify tactics, and look into new directions for success rather than as setbacks.

- **Learning Through Experimentation**

A mindset of experimentation and learning is fostered by a sense of comfort with uncertainty. Entrepreneurs understand that not all business endeavours will succeed immediately and that failure is a possible consequence. Rather than being afraid of failing, they see it as a source of insightful information that helps them to improve future attempts and strategies.

- **Staying Agile in a Changing Landscape**

The entrepreneurial environment is ever-changing due to the quick evolution of technologies, consumer behaviours, and market trends. In this ever-changing environment, entrepreneurs who are at ease with uncertainty remain adaptable.

They are quick to use new technologies, adjust to new trends, and get ahead of changes in the industry.

- **Maintaining Composure Under Pressure**

Stressful and stressful moments frequently result from uncertainty. These kinds of entrepreneurs remain calm in these kinds of situations. They perform well under pressure and take advantage of chances to demonstrate their adaptability, creativity, and ability to solve problems.

- **Strategic Decision-Making Amid Ambiguity**

Even in the face of ambiguity, entrepreneurs who are at ease with uncertainty make excellent strategic decisions. They gather the best available data, examine trends, and make decisions without waiting for perfect information. Their proactive strategy guarantees their leadership in a dynamic environment.

Chapter 4

<u>Why the Entrepreneurial Mindset Matters</u>

The first step to utilizing the entrepreneurial mind-sets' power is realizing its importance.

We'll go more deeply into the real-world uses of this mindset during this investigation, offering tips and techniques to support you as you embrace and develop these values on your own entrepreneurial path.

Think about the life-changing possibilities that come from adopting an entrepreneurial mindset and using it to advance both personally and professionally as we turn the pages ahead.

The capacity to think like an entrepreneur is a valuable asset in a landscape that is changing quickly and is highly competitive. Adopting this mindset can put you on the road to reaching your objectives and having a significant impact, regardless of whether you're an experienced business owner, an aspiring business owner, or someone who is just interested in the ideas behind successful entrepreneurship.

An essential aspect of the entrepreneurial mindset is embracing change and unpredictability. It is not only possible for entrepreneurs to survive in uncertain environments, but also to thrive in them when they are able to adapt to the changing business landscape and embrace the unknown. We will examine the theories and methods for handling uncertainty and change in this section.

- **Embracing Change and Uncertainty**

The entrepreneurial mindset offers a compass for navigating uncharted waters in a world where change is constant and uncertainty is the norm. Entrepreneurs thrive in uncertainty, not just survive it. People with an entrepreneurial mentality stay ahead of the curve by accepting change, changing quickly, and seeing opportunities where others see chaos.

One of the core principles of the entrepreneurial mindset is embracing change and uncertainty. It is not only possible for entrepreneurs to survive in uncertain environments, but also to thrive in them when they possess the adaptability and willingness to embrace the unknown necessary to navigate the ever-changing business landscape.

The ideas and tactics for accepting change and uncertainty will be discussed in this chapter.

- **Acceptance of the Inevitability of Change**

Entrepreneurs who adopt an open-minded attitude toward change understand that it is not only inevitable but also constant. They acknowledge that consumer preferences change, markets change, and technologies advance.

They can now view change as a chance for development and innovation rather than as a disruptive force because of their acceptance of it.

- **Cultivating a Positive Attitude Towards Uncertainty**

An optimistic outlook on uncertainty characterizes an entrepreneurial mindset. Entrepreneurs see uncertainty as a blank canvas for creativity and new possibilities, rather than as a cause of worry. They are able to tackle obstacles with hope, resiliency, and initiative thanks to this mentality change.

- **Agility in Decision-Making**

Adaptability in decision-making is necessary for embracing change. This kind of thinking makes entrepreneurs quick to modify their plans in light of fresh facts or changing conditions. They are aware that manoeuvring through uncertainty and establishing a strategic position for themselves in the market require swift action.

- **Continuous Learning and Adaptation**

Entrepreneurs who are dedicated to accepting change regard learning as an ongoing endeavour. They proactively search out new knowledge, keep up with market developments, and modify their expertise. They will stay adaptable and ready for any changes that the future may bring thanks to their dedication to lifelong learning.

- **Innovation as a Response to Change**

Innovation has many opportunities when things change. Owners who adopt this perspective use change as a spark for innovation and creativity. They actively look for ways to innovate goods, services, and business procedures rather than reacting to disruptions negatively in order to maintain their competitive edge in a market that is changing quickly.

- **Developing an Adaptive Culture**

Despite being a personal quality, building a team or organization culture that welcomes change is feasible. These business people put in a lot of effort to create a flexible environment.

To do this, motivate team members to embrace change as a whole, foster open communication, and cultivate a willingness to try new things.

Gaining an Advantage by Using Risk as a Tactic

Taking risks is embracing uncertainty on purpose. Entrepreneurs balance the pros and cons and take calculated risks when circumstances demand it. With their aptitude for seizing opportunities and setting themselves up for success when they can.

The Capacity to Learn from Mistakes

Setbacks could result from uncertainty, but flexible business people embrace change. Instead of seeing challenges as insurmountable, they see setbacks as transient hardships and opportunities for growth. They possess the fortitude to overcome obstacles, refine their tactics, and proceed without wavering.

Seeking Opportunities in Disruption

For those prepared to seize them, market disruptions frequently offer opportunities. Entrepreneurs are encouraged to actively seek out opportunities by using this way of thinking.

- **Encouraging Creativity and Innovation**

The heart of entrepreneurship is innovation. The entrepreneurial mindset promotes a continuous innovation and creative thinking culture. It inspires people to push the envelope of what is conceivable, seek out novel solutions, and question the status quo. This commitment to innovation drives industry advancement.

- **Acceptance of Change's Inevitability**

  Entrepreneurs who welcome change understand that it is both inevitable and constant. They understand that consumer preferences, technology advancements, and markets are dynamic. Their ability to accept change allows them to see it as an opportunity for advancement and creativity rather than as a dangerous force.

Cultivating a Positive Attitude Towards Uncertainty

The entrepreneurial mindset is characterized by a positive outlook on uncertainty. By contrast, entrepreneurs use uncertainty as a blank canvas for innovation and fresh ideas rather than as a cause for fear. By adopting this new perspective, individuals can tackle obstacles with a proactive, resilient, and upbeat attitude.

- **Agility in Decision-Making**

Adaptability in decision-making is necessary for embracing change. This kind of thinking makes entrepreneurs quick to modify their plans in light of fresh facts or changing conditions. They are aware that manoeuvring through uncertainty and establishing a strategic position for themselves in the market require swift action.

- **Continuous Learning and Adaptation**

Entrepreneurs who are dedicated to accepting change regard learning as an ongoing endeavour. They proactively search out new knowledge, keep up with market developments, and modify their expertise. They will stay adaptable and ready for any changes that the future may bring thanks to their dedication to lifelong learning.

- **Innovation as a Response to Change**

Innovation is frequently prompted by change. This kind of entrepreneur uses change as a spark for innovation and creativity. To stay ahead in a market that is changing quickly, they proactively look for ways to innovate their goods, services, and business procedures rather than reacting negatively to disruptions.

- **Building a Culture of Adaptability**

As a cultural quality that can be developed within a team or organization, accepting change is not just a personal characteristic. An adaptable culture is something that entrepreneurs with this mindset strive to create. As part of this, team members must be empowered to accept change as a group, have an open line of communication, and be willing to try new things.

- **Risk-Taking as a Strategic Approach**

Taking calculated risks is part of embracing uncertainty. When the circumstances call for it, entrepreneurs evaluate potential benefits against the risks and take measured chances. They are able to seize new opportunities and put themselves in a successful position by taking calculated risks, even in unsettling situations.

- **Resilience in the Face of Setbacks**

Setbacks can result from uncertainty, but resilient entrepreneurs embrace change in their thinking. Instead of seeing setbacks as insurmountable barriers, they see them as transient challenges and educational opportunities. Their capacity for resilience allows them to recover from setbacks, refine their tactics, and proceed with resoluteness.

- **Seeking Opportunities in Disruption**

Market disruptions frequently present opportunities for those prepared to take advantage of them. These types of entrepreneurs actively look for opportunities when things are changing. They are ready to take advantage of new needs and trends because they understand that times of change can also be times of great innovation.

Turning Challenges into Opportunities

The entrepreneurial mindset views obstacles as chances for development. Those who have this mindset view obstacles as opportunities to grow, change course, and learn rather than as something to be avoided. Resilience and determination are essential for conquering obstacles and turning them into opportunities for growth and achievement.

The capacity to convert obstacles into opportunities is one of the characteristics that characterize an entrepreneurial mindset. Entrepreneurs who see challenges as opportunities for learning, growth, and innovation rather than as barriers to overcome are better able to handle the intricacies of the business world. We'll look at the ideas and methods in this section for converting obstacles into opportunities.

Adopting a Solution-Oriented Mindset / Developing a Mindset Focused on Solutions

An entrepreneurial mindset is by its very nature solution-focused. Entrepreneurs take on challenges with a mindset that is centred on coming up with answers rather than moping over issues. They are able to evaluate circumstances impartially, recognize viable remedies, and act swiftly to overcome obstacles because of their proactive approach.

- **Embracing a Positive Attitude**

A positive attitude is an effective tool for turning obstacles into opportunities. Even in the face of adversity, entrepreneurs cultivate optimism. They are better able to see the silver lining in challenges and approach them with a can-do attitude, which fuels resilience and creative problem-solving when they maintain a positive mindset.

- **Seeking Learning and Growth**

People see challenges as chances for growth and learning. Entrepreneurs understand that every challenge is an opportunity to learn new things and gain new experiences, abilities, and insights. By viewing obstacles as teaching opportunities, they can continually change and adapt, which eventually improves their capacity for entrepreneurship.

- **Flexibility and Adaptability**

Adaptability and flexibility are essential qualities for converting obstacles into opportunities. When faced with unforeseen obstacles, entrepreneurs possess these qualities, which enable them to quickly pivot and modify their strategies.

This flexibility makes sure that obstacles don't stand in the way of advancement; rather, they serve as catalysts for creativity and evolution.

- **Innovative Problem-Solving**

Entrepreneurs take an inventive approach to problem-solving. They look for original and non-conventional ways to solve problems rather than depending just on traditional answers. This creative thinking creates new opportunities and future directions in addition to solving current problems.

- **Collaborative Problem-Solving**

Converting challenges into opportunities frequently necessitates teamwork. Entrepreneurs foster a collaborative culture by encouraging team members to share their insights and expertise in order to tackle challenges collectively. Collaborative problem-solving taps into the collective intelligence of the team, resulting in more robust solutions.

- **Agile Decision-Making**

When faced with a challenge, making quick decisions is critical. Entrepreneurs make quick and efficient decisions, adapting their strategies to changing circumstances.

Because of their agility, they are able to navigate challenges in a dynamic and responsive manner, seizing opportunities that may arise in the midst of uncertainty.

- **Strategic Risk-Taking**

Entrepreneurs are aware that taking calculated risks can pay off handsomely. They see obstacles as chances to carefully consider and take calculated risks that support their objectives. By taking calculated risks and exploring new ideas and avenues, they are able to turn obstacles into opportunities for growth and success.

- **Seeing Market Gaps and Needs**

Challenges frequently draw attention to market gaps and unmet needs. These gaps are closely watched by entrepreneurs, who view them as openings for creativity and business ventures. They not only overcome obstacles but also establish themselves as industry solution providers by attending to these needs.

Building Resilience Through Challenges

By facing challenges head-on, resilience is forged. It is common knowledge among entrepreneurs that facing challenges fosters perseverance and strength. Every obstacle they overcome successfully serves as evidence of their capacity to withstand adversity and come out on top—becoming more resilient, seasoned, and ready for new chances.

- **Building Resilience and Grit**

Developing grit and resilience is a key component of the entrepreneurial mindset. The ups and downs of the entrepreneurial journey are easier to handle for entrepreneurs who develop the resilience to overcome obstacles, persevere through setbacks, and pursue their goals with tenacity.

The journey of entrepreneurship is replete with ups and downs. The ability to be resilient and tenacious in the face of hardship is bestowed upon people who possess an entrepreneurial mindset. It's about persevering through setbacks, picking up lessons from past mistakes, and keeping up the will to work toward long-term objectives.

We'll look at the ideas and methods for developing grit and resilience in this section

1. **Understanding resilience:** The ability to overcome hardship, grow from errors, and emerge stronger is resilience. Resilient entrepreneurs see challenges not as insurmountable barriers to growth but as chances to grow. They overcome obstacles with grace, adjust to change, and view failures as opportunities for growth and progress in the future.

2. **Taking on an outlook that is growth-oriented**

The basis of resilience is a growth mindset. Growth-oriented entrepreneurs view obstacles as chances to grow and learn. Believing that their skills can be improved with dedication and hard work, they cultivate an attitude centred around lifelong learning and adaptability.

3. **Adopting a Growth Mindset**

The foundation of resilience is a growth mindset. Growing entrepreneurs see challenges as opportunities to develop and gain knowledge. Their belief that their abilities can be developed through hard work and dedication leads them to develop a mindset that thrives on continuous learning and adaptation.

4. **Resilience in the Face of Failures**

Grit, another word for perseverance, is the will to keep going after long-term objectives in the face of difficulty. Grit-filled entrepreneurs view obstacles as necessary stops along the way rather than as excuses to give up. In the face of hardship, they never waver from their objectives and persevere despite obstacles.

5. **Learning from Failure**

Failure is an unavoidable part of entrepreneurship, but resilient entrepreneurs use it as a learning experience. They objectively analyse failures, extract valuable insights, and use this knowledge to refine strategies.

Learning from failure helps to create a cycle of continuous improvement and boosts resilience.

6. Cultivating Emotional Intelligence

Resilience requires emotional intelligence. Entrepreneurs with high emotional intelligence effectively understand and manage their own emotions, as well as the emotions of others.

This ability enables them to maintain a balanced perspective during difficult times, make sound decisions, and form positive relationships.

7. Developing Coping Mechanisms

Developing effective coping mechanisms is part of the process of developing resilience. Entrepreneurs develop healthy coping mechanisms for stress, setbacks, and uncertainty. This could include practicing mindfulness, staying connected with others, or engaging in activities that provide a mental break and rejuvenation.

- **Setting Realistic Expectations**

Entrepreneurs who are resilient set realistic goals for themselves and their businesses. They recognize that challenges are unavoidable, and that success frequently entails overcoming obstacles. Entrepreneurs are better prepared to navigate the entrepreneurial journey with resilience if they set achievable goals and maintain a realistic outlook.

- **Building a Support Network**

One important tool for developing resilience is a solid support system. Entrepreneurs surround themselves with supportive networks, mentors, and advisors. This network builds a resilient mindset and offers support during trying times by offering advice, encouragement, and a sense of camaraderie.

- **Maintaining Physical and Mental Well-being**

Both mental and physical health are strongly correlated with resilience. Entrepreneurs place a high value on self-care, which includes stress reduction, consistent exercise, and enough sleep. The resilience of the body and mind required to face the challenges of entrepreneurship is enhanced by leading a healthy lifestyle.

- **Celebrating Small Wins**

Recognizing little victories is essential to developing resilience. Entrepreneurs encourage a positive outlook by recognizing and appreciating small victories. Acknowledging even the smallest amount of progress helps one feel accomplished and inspired to keep going in the face of obstacles in the future.

Fostering a Culture of Continuous Learning

The entrepreneurial mentality sees education as a continuous process. Entrepreneurs are lifelong learners who use experiences—both good and bad—to learn important lessons. They acquire knowledge from a variety of sources. People who are dedicated to lifelong learning are able to remain flexible and adaptive in a world that is changing quickly.

An essential component of the entrepreneurial mindset is promoting an environment that values lifelong learning. Entrepreneurs are better equipped to innovate, adapt to change, and stay ahead in a business environment that is changing quickly if they place a high priority on continuing education and foster a learning-oriented culture. We'll look at the ideas and tactics for creating a culture of lifelong learning in this section.

- **Setting an Example**

Entrepreneurs have a big influence on the organizational culture. By setting an exemplary example, displaying a dedication to learning, and actively pursuing new information, they establish the tone for a culture that values lifelong learning. An organization as a whole receives a clear message when leaders place a high priority on education.

- **Promoting Inquisitiveness and Research**

The cornerstone of a culture of continuous learning is curiosity. Within an environment that entrepreneurs foster, team members are encouraged to ask questions, seek understanding beyond their immediate responsibilities, and explore new ideas. Curiosity fuels this creative and dynamic approach.

- **Providing Learning Opportunities**

Entrepreneurs actively give their teams opportunities to learn. Programs for training, workshops, seminars, and access to educational materials fall under this category. Entrepreneurs who support their employees' professional growth not only help their staff members develop their own abilities but also add to the organization's collective knowledge base.

- **Supporting Professional Development**

One important facet of ongoing learning is professional development. By providing chances for skill development, going to conferences, getting certifications, and taking part in pertinent industry events, entrepreneurs help their team members advance professionally.

Both the organization and the individuals gain from this investment in professional development.

- **Embracing a Growth Mindset**

Being growth-oriented is essential for lifelong learning. Entrepreneurs foster and support a mentality that welcomes challenges, seizes the chance to learn, and views setbacks as chances for improvement.

This change in perspective encourages resilience and a culture where people are driven to reach their full potential.

- **Creating a Learning-Friendly Environment**

Entrepreneurs create environments in the workplace that support learning. This could entail setting up areas specifically for brainstorming and collaboration, giving people access to learning materials, and creating a welcoming environment where education is valued. A conducive learning environment promotes innovation and ongoing progress.

- **Promoting Cross-Functional Collaboration**

The confluence of various disciplines is often the thriving ground for continuous learning. Entrepreneurs encourage people from different departments to work together on projects by promoting cross-functional collaboration. This cooperative strategy encourages the sharing of ideas and knowledge, supporting an environment that values lifelong learning.

- **Recognizing and Celebrating Learning Achievements**

It's critical to recognize and celebrate learning successes. Entrepreneurs are aware of and appreciative of turning points in both individual and team learning. This acknowledgment encourages others to start their own educational endeavours by reiterating the importance of lifelong learning.

- **Establishing a Learning Feedback Loop**

Feedback is an effective instrument for growth and learning. Entrepreneurs create a loop for learning feedback in which learners receive helpful criticism on their efforts. This cycle, which fosters a culture of continuous improvement, consists of routine evaluations, conversations about advancement, and modifications to instructional techniques.

- **Emphasizing the Importance of Adaptability**

Adaptability and continuous learning are closely related. Entrepreneurs stress the value of flexibility and an open mind. To keep the company flexible and responsive to changing market conditions, team members are urged to adopt new technologies, procedures, and strategies.

<u>Cultivating a Proactive Approach</u>

There is no room for passivity in an entrepreneurial mindset. Rather, it advocates for a proactive method of resolving issues and establishing objectives. People who have this mentality actively seek out opportunities, seize them, and make them a reality rather than waiting for them to present themselves.

Developing a proactive mindset is a basic component of the entrepreneurial mindset. Instead of just responding to events, proactive entrepreneurs take the initiative, foresee obstacles, and actively shape their future.

We will delve into useful tactics for developing a proactive approach in both yourself and your team as we examine the entrepreneurial mindset. Adopting these values helps you establish a forward-thinking and proactive culture within your company, in addition to positioning yourself as a proactive entrepreneur.

Think about how developing a proactive mindset can help you approach opportunities and challenges differently and take your endeavours into new and unexplored areas.

- **Setting Clear Goals and Objectives**

The first step in a proactive approach is to clearly define goals and objectives. Entrepreneurs lay out their vision, convert it into attainable objectives, and create a plan of action to get there. Goal clarity offers a framework for guidance that facilitates proactive decision-making and strategic planning.

- **Anticipating Challenges and Opportunities**

Entrepreneurs that are proactive foresee obstacles and opportunities before they materialize. They practice strategic foresight, keeping abreast of market developments and identifying possible roadblocks. Being proactive in anticipating needs enables the creation of backup plans and puts the business owner in a position to react to changing conditions with effectiveness.

- **Taking Initiative and Ownership**

Taking initiative and taking ownership of one's actions are characteristics of being proactive. Instead of waiting for opportunities to present themselves, entrepreneurs actively seek them out and move quickly to seize them. People feel more accountable and responsible for the outcomes of their efforts when they take the initiative to do something.

- **Developing a Bias for Action**

The tendency toward action is what defines a proactive mindset. Acting is the only way to avoid missing opportunities, as entrepreneurs know. They are willing to iterate based on feedback, prioritize execution, and make decisions quickly. Ideas are translated into concrete outcomes thanks to this action-biasedness.

- **Continuous Learning and Skill Development**

People that are proactive make investments in their ongoing education and skill development. They broaden their skill set, learn new things, and remain up to date on developments in the industry. This dedication to lifelong learning guarantees that entrepreneurs are equipped to meet obstacles head-on and take advantage of new opportunities

- **Building a Network of Influence**

Entrepreneurs that take initiative create and utilize a network of influence. They actively work to build connections with peers, industry experts, mentors, and advisors. This network offers helpful information, encouragement, and chances for cooperation. Developing a robust network facilitates the proactive investigation of concepts and tactics.

- **Embracing Change and Innovation**

Embracing change and encouraging innovation are key components of a proactive strategy. An active pursuit of innovation in goods, services, and procedures characterizes entrepreneurs. They adjust to new developments in technology, shifting consumer behaviour, and changing market trends. Ventures can stay competitive and relevant by embracing change.

- **Effective Time Management**

Effective time management and proactivity go hand in hand. Entrepreneurs avoid procrastination, set deadlines, and prioritize tasks according to their strategic importance. This methodical approach to time management guarantees that important tasks are completed on time, which boosts productivity overall.

- **Cultivating Resilience in the Face of Setbacks**

People who take initiative develop resilience when faced with obstacles. They see obstacles as chances to develop and learn, and they remain optimistic in the face of hardship. Because of their resilience, entrepreneurs are able to overcome obstacles, modify their plans, and carry on.

- **Measuring and Analyzing Performance**

Regular performance measurement and analysis is a component of a proactive strategy. Entrepreneurs create key performance indicators (KPIs), monitor their progress, and assess how well their strategies are working. This ongoing evaluation enables modifications and enhancements, guaranteeing that the entrepreneurial path stays proactive.

Driving Personal and Professional Growth

The entrepreneurial mindset fosters personal development in areas other than business. It inspires people to step outside of their comfort zones, push boundaries, and realize unrealized potential. This way of thinking is about becoming a more resilient, creative, and contented person rather than just creating profitable businesses.

The entrepreneurial mindset is characterized by a constant pursuit of personal and professional development. Entrepreneurs who place a high priority on their own and their teams' personal growth lay the groundwork for long-term success.

We will examine the entrepreneurial mindset and discuss doable tactics to help you and your team grow personally and professionally. By adhering to these guidelines, you promote a continuous improvement and development culture within your company and establish yourself as a lifelong learner.

Think about how pursuing professional and personal growth can change the way you view opportunities and challenges and help you achieve greater success in your endeavours. This section will examine the ideas and tactics that promote both professional and personal development.

- **Setting Personal and Professional Development Goals**

Establishing specific, attainable goals for your professional and personal development is the first step on the path to growth. Entrepreneurs identify particular areas for growth in both their personal and professional lives. These objectives offer a path for ongoing improvement and learning.

- **Creating a Learning Plan**

Entrepreneurs create detailed learning plans that specify the actions needed to reach their expansion objectives. This plan might involve learning new skills, going after educational opportunities, going to conferences or workshops, and taking part in activities that advance one's career and personal development.

- **Seeking Mentorship and Guidance**

One of the most effective growth catalysts is mentoring. Entrepreneurs are always on the lookout for mentors who can offer direction, insights, and advice from their own experiences. Through the provision of insightful viewpoints and encouragement, mentoring relationships enhance both professional and personal development.

- **Embracing a Growth Mindset**

To promote both professional and personal growth, one must adopt a growth mindset. Entrepreneurs that have a growth mindset welcome the path of constant improvement, see obstacles as teaching opportunities, and have faith in their capacity to grow. Resilience and a proactive approach to growth are fostered by this mindset.

- **Networking and Relationship Building**

Developing a robust network is essential for both career and personal development. Entrepreneurs interact with peers, mentors, and professionals through networking opportunities and industry events. These connections offer perceptions, lead to opportunities, and advance knowledge of the business environment.

- **Balancing Work and Life**

Keeping a healthy work-life balance is essential for both professional and personal growth. Entrepreneurs understand the value of self-care, establishing limits, and scheduling personal activities. A well-rounded strategy improves productivity and resilience in both the personal and professional spheres, supporting general well-being.

- **Reflecting on Experiences and Learning**

Growth requires reflection, which is essential. Entrepreneurs routinely analyse their experiences—both triumphant and unsuccessful—in order to derive important insights. Reflective practice enables ongoing learning, strategy modification, and approach improvement for subsequent undertakings.

- **Staying Adaptable to Change**

A crucial quality for both professional and personal development is adaptability. Entrepreneurs maintain an open mind, seize new chances, and maintain their flexibility in the face of changing conditions. Their ability to adapt guarantees that they can profit from new trends and manoeuvre the ever-changing terrain of entrepreneurship.

- **Investing in Health and Well-being**

Physical and mental health are closely related to both professional and personal growth. Entrepreneurs put their health first by leading balanced lives, exercising frequently, getting enough sleep, and controlling their stress. Long-term energy and concentration are facilitated by a sound foundation.

- **Continuously Updating Skills and Knowledge**

Remaining current in a constantly changing setting necessitates regular skill and knowledge upgrades. Entrepreneurs actively look for chances to broaden their skill set, keep up with market trends, and value lifelong learning. Their dedication to remaining up to date improves their capacity to lead effectively and stimulate innovation.

- **Celebrating Milestones and Acknowledging Achievements**

Recognizing and appreciating progress along the way is essential to promoting both professional and personal growth.

Entrepreneurs celebrate their successes, no matter how small, as this uplifts the spirit and inspires continued growth. Honouring achievements encourages continued growth and helps one feel accomplished.

- **Creating Positive Impact**

Smart business people aim to improve their communities and the wider world in addition to pursuing success for their own benefit. The entrepreneurial mindset encourages people to start businesses that advance societal well-being by instilling in them a sense of accountability and purpose.

The Journey Ahead

This chapter will explore the essential elements of the entrepreneurial mindset and the characteristics that enable people to transform ideas into reality. Every aspect—from creativity and resilience to risk-taking and adaptability—contributes significantly to forming the mindset that drives entrepreneurial endeavours.

The path of an entrepreneur is a never-ending adventure characterized by development, difficulties, and constant learning. The following guidelines and tactics should be taken into account as you set out on your journey in order to handle the challenges of entrepreneurship with fortitude, inventiveness, and a forward-thinking outlook.

1. Embrace Uncertainty

See uncertainty as a blank canvas waiting to be explored and innovated upon, rather than as a barrier. Accept change and approach the unknown with curiosity and initiative, realizing that opportunities frequently present themselves when things are changing.

2. Learn from Setbacks

Failures are not impediments to achievement, but rather stepping stones. Accept failure as a potent teacher, draw insightful conclusions, and utilize every experience to hone your tactics and methods.

3. Cultivate Adaptability

One of the characteristics of successful entrepreneurs is flexibility. Maintain an adaptable mindset in the face of change, keep learning new things, and cultivate an innovative and flexible team culture.

4. Prioritize Relationships

Establishing solid relationships is essential for success. Build a support system of mentors, collaborators, and allies who can help you grow both personally and professionally by offering advice and insights.

5. Nurture a Culture of Innovation

Promote innovation by cultivating an environment that values diversity of thought, accepts change, and stimulates creativity. proactively look for ways to innovate your goods, services, and operational procedures.

6. Maintain a Long-Term Perspective

As you navigate the challenges of the day, keep an eye on the future. Develop a long-term outlook, specific objectives, and tactics that support the long-term viability and sustainability of your endeavours.

7. Balance Ambition with Realism

Set high standards for yourself, but keep them in check by acknowledging the difficulties you may face. Strike a balance between aspiration and pragmatism so that your goals are in line with realistic timetables and steps.

8. Foster a Culture of Continuous Learning

Make learning a lifelong endeavour your top priority. Establish a culture in your team where ongoing education is valued, make educational investments, and set a positive example for others by committing to both your professional and personal development.

9. Utilize the Power of Resilience

Make resilience a necessary quality. Accept obstacles as chances to get stronger, keep a positive outlook in the face of failure, and utilize adversity as a springboard for your professional and personal growth.

10. Honour significant anniversaries

Along the way, acknowledge and celebrate your accomplishments. No matter how small, celebrating your successes lifts your spirits, maintains a positive attitude, and gives you the motivation to tackle the next set of challenges.

11. Lead with Purpose and Vision

Clearly articulate the objectives and vision you have for your work. Give your team a shared goal that is meaningful and goes beyond financial gain to inspire them. This will support each team member's motivation and attention span.

12. Adapt and Evolve

Being an entrepreneur is a dynamic journey that calls for ongoing adjustment. Be prepared to adjust your tactics as needed and to keep an eye on how your industry is developing.

Keep in mind that every step you take on the journey ahead presents an opportunity for impact, growth, and innovation.

Realizing Potential

As we delve into the entrepreneurial mindset, take this as a chance to think about your own goals, obstacles, and lost opportunities. The ideas covered here can act as a roadmap to help you discover your natural entrepreneurial spirit, whether you're launching a company, managing a team, or looking for personal development.

Reaching the maximum potential in your business ventures requires a deliberate and methodical approach.

Take into account the following guidelines and tactics as you set out to maximize your potential:

- **Clarify Your Vision**

Establish a compelling and unambiguous vision for your endeavours. Clearly state your goals and the kind of impact you hope to achieve.

A clear vision acts as a beacon of light, directing your team's efforts and your own toward a common goal.

- **Identify Core Competencies**

Recognize your main skills and areas of strength. Determine the special abilities, resources, and skills that make you stand out. By making the most of these advantages, you can gain a competitive edge and take a calculated stand in the marketplace.

- **Set Ambitious Goals**

Create tough but reachable goals that complement your vision. Break larger objectives down into smaller, more achievable goals. Ambitious goals encourage constant improvement by forcing you to step outside of your comfort zone.

- **Always Be Inventive**

Innovation is a key component of potential realization. Promote a continuous innovation culture within your organization. Encourage creative thinking, embrace cutting-edge technology, and stay ahead of market trends if you want to remain relevant and competitive.

- **Invest in Talent Development**

Building a team is crucial to realizing your potential. It is an investment in your team members' professional development to provide them with growth, mentoring, and training opportunities. An accomplished team helps the business reach its goals and boosts overall output.

- **Create Strategic Alliances**

Look into strategic partnerships to fill in any skill gaps and strengthen your advantages. Reaching your full potential and opening up new possibilities for growth and creativity can be achieved by collaborating with other businesses, organizations, or people.

- **Leverage Technology**

Recognize technology as a catalyst for growth and productivity. Select and put into use technologies that increase output, streamline processes, and provide useful data. Technology can help you realize your full potential and accomplish your goals.

- **Keep an eye on KPIs, or key performance indicators**

Select and regularly monitor key performance indicators (KPIs) that are relevant to your objectives. KPIs provide measurable benchmarks that enable you to track your

 progress, spot problem areas, and make data-driven choices to maximize performance.

- **Maintain Customer-Centricity**

Give a customer-focused strategy top precedence. Acknowledge the needs, inclinations, and opinions of your clients. You can increase customer satisfaction and create advocates who support you in realizing your full potential by going above and beyond what the customer expects and providing value.

- **Gain Knowledge from Comments/ feedbacks**

Consult with a variety of people, including customers, team members, and mentors. Constructive feedback provides valuable insights for enhancement and optimization. To enhance and modify your strategies, use feedback as a continuous feedback loop.

- **Foster a Culture of Excellence**

Establish an excellence-focused culture in your company. Establish strict guidelines for output, calibre, and client support. Promote a culture of continuous improvement in which all team members are dedicated to reaching the highest standards in their specialized roles.

- **Adapt to Changing Conditions**

Potential realization necessitates flexibility. Keep an eye out for external variables that could affect your business endeavours as well as market trends and shifting consumer behaviour. Be open to changing your tactics and methods in order to effectively navigate changing circumstances.

- **Celebrate Achievements**

Celebrate and honour your accomplishments and landmarks along the road. Acknowledging accomplishments, no matter how small, promotes a happy and driven workplace. Recalling accomplishments through celebration motivates continued work toward possible realization.

The Entrepreneurial Mindset in Action

The background and inspiration for this lesson will come from actual individuals who have demonstrated the entrepreneurial mindset. These stories illustrate the transformative power of embracing fresh viewpoints, rising to obstacles, and pursuing objectives with ardour and resolve.

The entrepreneurial mindset cannot be realized unless ideas are translated into workable strategies. When you use the entrepreneurial mindset to inspire creativity, resilience, and innovation in your endeavour's, keep in mind these achievable steps:

1. **Cultivate Curiosity**

Encourage a culture of inquiry among your employees. Plan brainstorming sessions, encourage inquiry, and establish an environment that values new ideas. Seek out opposing perspectives to promote original thought.

2. **Strengthen Decision-Making**

Allow your employees to take ownership of the projects they work on and make their own decisions. Create a framework for decision-making, encourage taking calculated risks, and cultivate an atmosphere where individuals feel free to express their ideas and take the initiative.

3. **Encourage educational opportunities**

Make a constant effort to offer learning opportunities to your team and to yourself. This may include training sessions, conferences, and workshops. To make sure your knowledge and abilities are current, stay up to date on industry trends and emerging technologies.

4. Encourage Iterative Problem-Solving

Foster a mindset of iterative problem-solving. Instead of viewing challenges as roadblocks, encourage your team to see them as opportunities for improvement. Iterate on solutions, learn from each iteration, and continuously refine your approaches.

5. Build Cross-Functional Collaboration

Encourage cooperation between team members who perform different tasks. Interdepartmental cooperation promotes the sharing of concepts, viewpoints, and knowledge.

This kind of teamwork can result in creative fixes and a more comprehensive comprehension of problems.

6. Create an Inclusive Environment

Create a welcoming atmosphere where each team member is respected and heard. Diversity in perspective and experience can enhance the overall quality of ideas and promote an innovative and creative culture.

7. Lead with Vision

Make your future vision clear to everyone. Motivate your group by discussing the bigger picture and the effects of your projects. A compelling vision inspires people to work together toward a common goal, which inspires them to give it their all.

8. Encourage Risk-Taking

Establish a secure environment for measured risk-taking. Even if a new idea involves some degree of uncertainty, encourage your team to investigate it. Taking measured risks is a necessary component of innovation and growth.

9. Celebrate Small Wins

Celebrate each little accomplishment you make along the way. Acknowledging successes—no matter how small—raises spirits and highlights the beneficial effects of both individual and group efforts. Festivity fosters an environment of gratitude and inspiration.

10. Embrace Change

Establish a mindset that welcomes change. Assist your team in viewing change as a chance for development and adaptation rather than as a threat. Promote adaptability and a proactive attitude toward change to keep your endeavours nimble and responsive.

11. Grant Ownership and Independence

Give your team members freedom and responsibility for the job they do. People are more likely to be proactive, show initiative, and contribute to the overall success of the company when they have a sense of ownership.

12. Adapt and Pivot Strategically

Be ready to strategically change course and adapt. Continually evaluate market conditions, stakeholder feedback, and the external environment. Make well-informed decisions to adjust your strategies as needed to account for evolving conditions.

13. Foster a Growth Mindset

Encourage a growth mentality in every department of your company. Promote the idea that skills can be acquired with commitment and effort. Resilience, a love of learning, and an openness to accepting new experiences are all fostered by a growth mindset.

14. Invest in Team Well-being

Acknowledge the role that wellbeing plays in motivating performance. Invest in programs that enhance your team's mental and physical health. A team that is motivated and in good health is more likely to help your endeavour's succeed.

15. Lead by Example

In your leadership, set an example of an entrepreneurial mindset. Exhibit a dedication to lifelong learning, fortitude in the face of difficulty, and a proactive spirit when it comes to innovation. The tone of the entire organization is set by those who lead by example.

It takes deliberate work and a dedication to promoting a culture of creativity, resilience, and continuous improvement to put the entrepreneurial mindset into practice.

Chapter 5

The Importance of Entrepreneurship

The engine of innovation, economic expansion, and societal advancement is entrepreneurship. The following are some major points that emphasize how important entrepreneurship is:

- **Innovation and Creativity**

Entrepreneurs are at the forefront of innovation, introducing new products, services, and business models. Their creative thinking and willingness to take risks contribute to technological advancements and improved ways of solving problems.

- **Economic Growth and Job Creation**

Economic growth is greatly aided by small and medium-sized enterprises (SMEs), many of which are led by entrepreneurs. In addition to boosting local economies and opening up job opportunities, they also advance overall economic growth.

- **Adaptability and Resilience**

The qualities of resilience and adaptability that entrepreneurs exemplify are crucial for navigating quickly evolving business environments. The development of markets and industries is fuelled by their capacity to change course, take calculated risks, and endure in the face of difficulties.

- **Wealth Creation and Prosperity**

Entrepreneurial endeavours possess the capacity to produce wealth for the business owners, as well as for their staff and the communities in which they operate. Entrepreneurs who are successful can spread prosperity on many levels by starting a positive chain reaction.

- **Job Market Diversity**

A variety of business ideas and opportunities are introduced by entrepreneurship, which adds to the diversity of the labour market. With so many different industries and career paths to choose from, diversity is essential for a vibrant and competitive labour market.

- **Social Impact and Problem Solving**

A common motivation for entrepreneurs is to solve societal issues. By creating solutions for issues pertaining to healthcare, education, the environment, or other pressing concerns, their endeavours have a positive social impact.

- **Fostering a Culture of Innovation**

Innovation is encouraged by the entrepreneurial spirit not just in individual businesses but also in other sectors of the economy. It promotes an attitude of constant improvement, flexibility in the face of change, and an openness to considering novel approaches.

- **Global Competitiveness**

By encouraging an environment of creativity and productivity, entrepreneurial endeavors improve a nation's ability to compete internationally. A country's ability to compete in the international market is frequently enhanced by its encouragement and support of entrepreneurship.

- **Ecosystem Development**

New businesses, investors, mentors, and support groups work together in dynamic ecosystems that are fostered by entrepreneurship. Access to resources, networking, and information sharing are made easier by these ecosystems, which are frequently present in entrepreneurial hubs.

- **Encouraging Self-Empowerment**

People who are entrepreneurial are able to take charge of their lives, follow their passions, and make their own opportunities. It promotes independence, self-sufficiency, and a feeling of control over one's career path.

- **Cultural and Social Change**

Entrepreneurial ventures can bring about cultural and social change by challenging existing norms and introducing innovative ideas. Entrepreneurs often lead movements that reshape industries and influence societal attitudes.

- **Technological Advancements**

Innovations in technology are largely the result of entrepreneurial endeavour's. Entrepreneurs, whether they run start-up businesses or well-established tech firms, frequently lead the way in innovations that fundamentally alter the way we communicate, work, and live.

To sum up, entrepreneurship is a key factor in societal transformation, economic growth, and progress. It empowers people, encourages innovation, and advances the prosperity of communities and countries. Encouraging and recognizing entrepreneurship's value is crucial to creating societies that are resilient, vibrant, and progressive.

Characteristics of Successful Entrepreneurs

There are certain traits that successful business owners have in common that help them overcome obstacles, think creatively, and create profitable enterprises.

All of these qualities work together to make entrepreneurs successful. The combination of vision, passion, adaptability, and a proactive mindset sets apart successful entrepreneurs, even though individual entrepreneurs may have these qualities to differing degrees.

The following are essential traits of prosperous business people:

- **Visionary Thinking**

Entrepreneurs that are successful have a distinct goal in mind. They have the ability to look ahead and imagine how their businesses, industries, or even society will develop. Their strategic decisions and actions are guided by this visionary thinking.

- **Passion and Determination**

A key motivator for entrepreneurs is passion. People who are successful have a strong sense of passion for what they do, and this passion drives them to overcome challenges. Despite obstacles, they never waver in their commitment to their objectives.

- **Adaptability and Flexibility**

Successful business people are flexible and able to adjust to the ever-changing business environment. They welcome change, modify their plans as needed, and remain nimble in the face of unforeseen obstacles or shifting market conditions.

- **Innovative Thinking**

The secret to successful entrepreneurship is innovation. Entrepreneurs that are successful are innovative thinkers who are always looking for new and improved methods to accomplish tasks. They are willing to question the status quo and investigate novel concepts.

- **Resourcefulness**

Entrepreneurs that are successful are resourceful in making the most of what is available to them. They find innovative solutions and make the most of their resources—financial, human, or technological—to accomplish their goals.

- **Risk-Taking**

Risk is a necessary part of entrepreneurship, and successful business people aren't afraid to take measured chances. They evaluate possible results, make defensible choices, and accept risk as a necessary component of development and creativity.

- **Long-Term Perspective**

Entrepreneurs that are successful have a long-term outlook. They are not only motivated by short-term profits, but also concentrate on creating sustainable businesses. Their strategic planning and decision-making are informed by this viewpoint.

- **Proactive Problem-Solving**

Successful entrepreneurs are proactive in resolving issues, and they face a variety of obstacles. Rather than waiting for problems to get worse, they proactively look for answers, modify their strategies, and take lessons from mistakes.

- **Comfort with Uncertainty**

Because starting a business involves a lot of uncertainty, successful business people are accustomed to working in this setting. They are able to negotiate uncertainty, make choices without all the facts, and adapt to unanticipated events.

- **Strong Work Ethic**

Prosperous business people are renowned for their diligent work ethics. They work assiduously, are committed, and frequently put in long hours to make sure their endeavour's succeed. Among them, a dedication to excellence and tenacity are characteristic.

- **Effective Communication Skills**

Establishing partnerships, leading teams, and fostering relationships all depend on effective communication. Entrepreneurs who are successful are able to express their ideas clearly, close deals, and motivate others because they have good communication skills.

- **Emphasis on the Customer**

Consumers are the top priority for successful business owners. They actively seek feedback, are aware of the needs of their customers, and work to provide value. Positive brand perception and customer loyalty are facilitated by a customer-centric approach.

- **Building Relationships and Networking**

The key to a successful business is building a network of contacts. Successful businesspeople follow these strategies: they network, look for mentors, and build strong relationships within their industries. Cooperation and new opportunities are often the result of these connections.

- **Continuous Learning**

Successful entrepreneurs are dedicated to lifelong learning because the business environment is ever-changing. They devote time to their professional and personal development, learn new skills, and remain up to date on industry trends.

- **Resilience and Grit:**

Entrepreneurship entails overcoming obstacles and failing. Resilience and grit are traits of successful entrepreneurs; they overcome obstacles, grow from setbacks, and remain optimistic in the face of difficulty.

Identifying Opportunities

One of the most important aspects of entrepreneurship is opportunity identification, which calls for a blend of strategic thinking, market knowledge, and creativity.

The following techniques can assist you in spotting potential business ventures:

1. **Stay Informed About Industry Trends**

Stay up to date on industry trends by conducting regular research. This covers modifications to consumer behaviour, the emergence of new technologies, and adjustments to market dynamics. Recognizing patterns can assist you in finding openings and gaps.

2. **Understand Customer Needs**

To comprehend the requirements and inclinations of your intended audience, conduct in-depth market research. Determine the problems and difficulties they encounter, then investigate creative ways to meet those needs.

3. Network and Build Relationships

One effective strategy for finding opportunities is networking. Participate in industry events, network with professionals, and form bonds with other business owners. Networking can lead to insights, partnerships, and possible business ventures.

4. Solve Problems

Determine whether there are any issues or inefficiencies in the market and investigate potential solutions. The identification and resolution of customer pain points is a common pathway to successful business ventures.

5. Examine Emerging Technologies

Be mindful of the latest technological advancements and their potential applications across diverse sectors. Blockchain technology, artificial intelligence, and the Internet are a few examples of the digital innovations that can be made possible.

6. Keep an open mind and remain curious

As you approach your surroundings, remain open-minded and attentive. Being receptive to new perspectives and ideas can yield innovative insights that others might overlook. Unexpected opportunities can also arise.

7. Keep tabs on rivals

Check for any holes in the market or areas where you can differentiate yourself by examining the goods and services offered by your competitors. Being aware of competitors' benefits and drawbacks can help you position your business profitably.

8. Evaluate Your Skills and Interests

Think about your own abilities, knowledge, and passions. Seek opportunities where you can use your special skills and that are in line with your passions. Expertise and passion can be effective motivators for achievement.

9. Leverage Your Network

Ask those in your network for advice and inspiration. Speaking with mentors, co-workers, and business experts about prospective opportunities can yield a variety of viewpoints and insightful discussions.

10. Explore Global Markets

Look into opportunities in countries other than your own. There might be specific needs and gaps in international markets that your goods and services can fill. Take into account the prospects for growth and globalization.

11. Observe Consumer Behaviour

Pay attention to how consumers behave and the patterns they exhibit. Changes in behaviour can signal emerging opportunities. This includes shifts in preferences, purchasing habits, and the adoption of new technologies.

12. Evaluate Regulatory Changes

Modifications to laws or policies have the power to transform markets and reshape established sectors. Keep up with any legislative developments that might have an effect on your industry, and consider how you might benefit from or adjust to these changes.

13. Attend Trade Shows and Conferences

Take part in conferences and trade exhibits tailored to your industry. Exposure to the newest innovations, trends, and opportunities is offered by these events. Making connections with experts in your industry can yield insightful information.

14. Think Beyond the Obvious

Push yourself to think outside the box and consider opportunities that may seem obvious. Think about joint ventures, related industries, or unorthodox approaches to issues. The most prosperous businesspeople frequently spot opportunities where others see obstacles.

15. Identify Unmet Needs

Seek out areas of the market with gaps where needs are not being sufficiently met. Finding unmet needs or gaps in the current solutions often leads to opportunities.

Keep in mind that seeing opportunities is a continuous process that calls for a blend of creativity, analysis, and observation. Remain inquisitive, adjust to shifts, and take the initiative to investigate new opportunities for your business endeavour's.

Chapter 6

The Role of Mindset in Business Success:

As we delve deeper, we'll look at how entrepreneurial mind-sets affect the success of companies. Expanding, being creative, and being successful over the long haul are all possible with the right mindset, regardless of experience level or type of business owner.

The attitude you bring to the table is a critical component in deciding how successful your business will be. This piece looks at the key elements of mindset and how they impact the trajectory of your business endeavour's.

1. The Power of Belief

Your self-belief, your endeavour's, and your capacity for overcoming obstacles are fundamental. The resilience and tenacity required to handle the highs and lows of entrepreneurship are fostered by a positive and self-assured mindset.

2. Innovation and Adaptability

Having an entrepreneurial mindset promotes creativity and flexibility. A mindset that enables businesses to not only survive in dynamic environments, but to thrive there requires embracing change, looking for innovative solutions, and staying ahead of industry trends.

3. Risk-Taking and Fear of Failure

An essential component of business success is the ability to take measured risks. Having an entrepreneurial mindset makes it possible to overcome your fear of failing and see failures as chances for personal development rather than insurmountable challenges.

4. Problem-Solving Orientation

Problem-solving entrepreneurs view obstacles as puzzles to be solved rather than impediments. This way of thinking promotes proactive problem-solving and a continuous improvement culture within the company.

5. Vision and Goal Alignment

A success-oriented mindset is built on a foundation of a well-defined vision and goals. Entrepreneurs who possess a strategic vision are able to direct their team's efforts and their own toward a shared goal, leading the company toward long-term success.

6. Customer-Centric Focus

One of the characteristics of a customer-centric mindset is giving the needs and satisfaction of the customer priority. This approach helps you establish trusting connections, encourage client loyalty, and improve your company's reputation.

7. Learning and Adaptation

Continuous learning is highly valued in an entrepreneurial mindset. In order to remain competitive and relevant, you must be willing to learn new skills, keep up with industry advancements, and modify your plans in response to criticism.

8. Resilience in the Face of Setbacks

One essential quality of prosperous businesspeople is resilience. Maintaining momentum and conquering obstacles requires the capacity to recover from setbacks, learn from mistakes, and keep a positive outlook under trying circumstances.

9. Collaboration and Team Building

Collaborative entrepreneurs recognize and value their team members' contributions. The success of the company as a whole is influenced by creating a solid and cohesive team, promoting teamwork, and identifying individual strengths.

10. Focus on Value Creation

An entrepreneurial mindset prioritizes adding value over maximizing profits. Entrepreneurs who are successful are driven by a desire to solve problems for their clients, make a positive impact, and meaningfully impact the communities they serve.

11. Getting Ready for Market Trends

Remaining up to date with consumer and market trends is essential for business success. By proactively modifying your offerings and strategies in response to shifting market dynamics, you can assure long-term relevance by adopting an entrepreneurial mindset.

12. Long-Term Outlook

For a business to succeed, having a long-term perspective is frequently essential. Thinking ahead, forward-thinking entrepreneurs plan for the future, strategically allocate their funds, and establish their businesses for sustained success.

13. Embracing Challenges as Opportunities

Entrepreneurship is full of challenges, but how you approach them depends on your mentality. When obstacles are seen as chances for development, education, and creativity, hardship can be turned into a success-boosting force.

14. Networking and Relationship Building

Success as an entrepreneur is frequently correlated with networking and developing relationships. One can discover opportunities, insights, and collaborative opportunities by adopting a mindset that values connections, actively seeks mentorship, and cultivates a network of support.

15. Celebrating Achievements

Taking time to acknowledge and celebrate achievements is crucial for maintaining motivation and morale. An entrepreneurial mindset appreciates the journey, recognizes milestones, and uses positive reinforcement to inspire ongoing efforts.

To put it briefly, there are many different aspects to mind-sets' role in business success. It shapes your decision-making process, approach to problems, and organizational culture. You lay the groundwork for both attaining business success and living out your entrepreneurial dreams by cultivating an optimistic, creative, and resilient state of mind.

Real-world Examples of Entrepreneurs with a Strong Mindset

Inspiring real-world entrepreneurs who have exhibited a strong entrepreneurial mindset will be our source of motivation throughout this chapter. These people have made an enduring impact on the business world by overcoming difficulties, accepting failure, and turning problems into opportunities.

These are actual cases of business owners who have bravely faced challenges with a positive outlook and creative ideas.

We will take our cues from successful real-world entrepreneurs who have exhibited a strong entrepreneurial mindset throughout this chapter. By overcoming difficulties, accepting failure, and converting obstacles into opportunities, these people have made a lasting impression on the business community.

Here are some real-life instances of business owners who have persevered, had a positive outlook, and used creativity in their thinking:

1. Elon Musk (Tesla, SpaceX, Neuralink, and more)
    - **Mindset Traits**: Musk is renowned for his audacious plans, daring ventures, and unwavering pursuit of objectives. Despite a great deal of opposition, financial difficulties, and doubt, he has persisted in pushing the frontiers of innovation in renewable energy, electric vehicles, and space travel.
2. Oprah Winfrey (OWN Network, Harpo Productions)
    - **Mindset Qualities**: Oprah's resilience, optimistic outlook, and dedication to self-improvement are credited with her success. She overcame hardship early in her career to create a media empire, proving the value of sincerity, compassion, and lifelong learning.
3. Richard Branson (Virgin Group)
    - **Mindset Traits**: Fearlessness, adaptability, and a willingness to take chances are evident in Branson's entrepreneurial journey. Virgin was founded by him as a modest mail-order record company, and it grew into a broad range of industries, including music, space exploration, aviation, and telecommunications.
4. Sara Blakely (Spanx)
    - **Mindset Traits**: Blakely's entrepreneurial journey started because she had a great belief in her concept and was prepared to stick with it in the face of many rejections. She founded the ground-breaking underwear brand Spanx and went on to become one of the youngest female self-made billionaires.
5. Jack Ma (Alibaba Group)

- **Mindset Traits**: Resilience, flexibility, and a clear vision for the future of e-commerce are the cornerstones of Jack Ma's success. He overcame early setbacks and rejections to create Alibaba, the world's largest online retailer, by navigating challenging markets and encouraging creativity.

6. Steve Jobs (Apple Inc.):
   - **Mindset Traits:** Industry disruptor, innovator, and unwavering perfectionist Steve Jobs was well-known for. Even though he encountered obstacles, he managed to turn Apple into one of the most significant technology businesses in the world by launching ground-breaking devices like the iPad and iPhone.

7. Arianna Huffington (Huff Post, Thrive Global)
   - **Mindset Traits:** Huffington has demonstrated perseverance and a dedication to wellbeing throughout her journey. She overcame obstacles to found HuffPost, a ground-breaking online news outlet, and subsequently Thrive Global, a company that promotes mindfulness and balance in the workplace.

8. Mark Zuckerberg (Facebook)
   - **Mindset Traits**: The bold vision and adaptability of Zuckerberg's approach set it apart. In his college dorm room, he created Facebook. He overcame challenges, took the platform global, and kept the company at the forefront of technological and social media changes.

9. Bill & Melinda Gates Foundation's Melinda Gates
   - **Mindset Traits**: Melinda Gates is one person who emphasizes innovation, philanthropy, and having a positive social impact. She co-chairs the Bill & Melinda Gates Foundation with her ex-husband Bill Gates, addressing global health, education, and poverty issues.

10. Tony Robbins, a motivational speaker and entrepreneur
    - **Mindset Traits:** Tony Robbins is well-known for his ability to motivate people and for his perseverance and upbeat outlook. He overcame personal obstacles to become a prosperous businessman, life coach, and motivational speaker who inspired millions of people to succeed in both their personal and professional lives.

These business owners have a diverse range of success stories, but they all possess a strong work ethic, flexibility, perseverance, and a resolve to stick with their goals even in the face of challenges. Their experiences can serve as an inspiration to prospective business owners who are seeking guidance on overcoming obstacles in the course of launching and expanding profitable ventures.

Chapter 7

Finding Your Niche

Finding your niche allows you to concentrate on a specific market segment and differentiate your goods or services, which is crucial for entrepreneurs. You can follow these steps to determine and define your niche:

- **Self-Reflection**

Start by thinking about your own interests, talents, and passions. Regarding what do you truly get excited? Assessing your own interests and strengths can help you find a niche that aligns with your abilities and interests.

- **Determine Any Market Gaps**

Look over the market to identify any gaps or underserved areas. Look for needs that are not adequately met by the products and services that are currently available. These gaps might offer opportunities for you to establish a market niche by providing unique solutions.

- **Investigate Your Target Audience**

Gain a comprehensive grasp of your intended audience. Market research is necessary to identify specific pain points, preferences, and demographics. Tailor your specialty to the particular needs and tastes of your target market.

- **Examine Your Rivals**

Look into the services provided by your competitors to see if they are providing enough for their customers. Try to find ways to differentiate yourself from the competitors by providing better, more specialized services or serving a specific customer base.

- **Think About Your UVP, or Unique Value Proposition**

Explain your unique value proposition, or UVP. What sets your product apart from rivals in the market? You can carve out a distinct niche for yourself by highlighting a unique selling point for your good or service.

Assess Trends and Industry Transitions

Stay up to date on developments and trends within the sector. New trends could point to opportunities in specialized markets. Think about how you can modify your business to align with these trends or cater to a specific market segment in the dynamic landscape.

- **Assess Your Expertise**

Think about your own knowledge and background. What qualifications or expertise do you have that will help you stand out? Your knowledge may serve as the basis for a specialty market in which you can offer unique benefits.

- **Test and Validate**

Test your niche concept to ensure there is a market for it. Conduct surveys, solicit feedback, or launch a pilot to determine whether your niche idea is appealing to your target audience. Adapt your strategy in response to feedback.

- **Examine Micro-Niches**

Look into the niches of smaller markets. Consider focusing on a specific subgroup with specific needs rather than trying to reach a large audience. Where there is less competition, micro-niches may offer more specialized solutions.

• **Profitability Assessment**

Analyse the profitability potential of your niche. Consider factors such as the size of the market, the purchasing power of the target audience, and the degree of competition. Verify if your niche can sustainably grow your company financially.

- **Leverage Your Network**

Make use of your professional and personal networks to gain insights. Talk about your niche ideas with mentors, colleagues, and industry experts to get different perspectives and valuable feedback.

- **Stay Flexible and Adapt**

Be willing to change your niche in response to market feedback and changing dynamics. Market conditions may change, and your adaptability ensures that your niche remains relevant.

- **Evaluate Legal and Regulatory Considerations**

Think about any restrictions or laws that apply to your niche. Make sure the niche you've selected complies with industry rules and that you are aware of any particular legal requirements.

Define Your Brand Identity

Your brand identity should be consistent with your niche. Establish the image and values that you want to be associated with your brand in the selected niche. Maintaining a consistent brand enhances your standing in the industry.

- **Test Marketing Strategies**

Try out various marketing techniques to reach your target audience before settling on a niche. Analyse these tactics' efficacy and adjust your strategy in light of the findings.

Discovering your specialty is a continuous process that calls for a harmony of imagination, ingenuity, and flexibility. You can position your company for success in a market niche that plays to your strengths and caters to the particular needs of your target clientele by carefully identifying your niche.

Chapter 8

Market Research and Analysis: A Comprehensive Guide

Conducting market research and analysis is essential for launching and growing a profitable company. They provide incisive details about market dynamics, competitive settings, and consumer behaviour. This comprehensive guide will help you conduct effective market research and analysis.

- **Establish Your Goals**

Clearly identify the objectives that your market research will seek to achieve. Are you launching a new product, entering a new market, or assessing how satisfied customers are? Your particular objectives will direct your research strategy.

- **Determine Who Your Target Market Is**

Ascertain the characteristics, preferences, and actions of your intended audience. It will be easier for you to concentrate your research and gather relevant data if you know who your ideal client is.

- **Choose Research Methods**

Choosing the right research techniques depends on your goals. Data analysis, focus groups, surveys, interviews, and observational studies are examples of common techniques. Using a variety of approaches yields a more complete picture.

- **Conduct Competitor Analysis**

Analyse rivals to learn about their advantages, disadvantages, positioning in the market, and views of the public. Determine the market gaps and opportunities for offering differentiation.

- **SWOT Analysis**

Analyse your company's SWOT (Strengths, Weaknesses, Opportunities, and Threats). Potential growth areas and areas for improvement are identified with the aid of this internal and external assessment.

- **Analyse Industry Trends**

Keep up with changes in regulations, technology, and industry trends. This information guarantees that your company stays competitive and in step with the changing market environment.

- **Gather Primary Data**

Ask the individuals you wish to reach for first-hand primary data. This can be accomplished through focus groups, interviews, and surveys. Make sure your inquiries are well-written to get intelligent answers.

- **Utilize Secondary Source Information**

Make use of the data that is already accessible through publications from government agencies, trade journals, and academic institutions. Understanding competitor landscapes, market sizes, and trends is made easier with the help of secondary data.

- **Examine client testimonials and feedback**

Examine customer endorsements, remarks, and comments on social media about your industry or competitors. Information regarding issues and customer satisfaction is provided by this qualitative data.

- **Assess Pricing Strategies**

Look into the pricing strategies employed in your industry. Analyse what consumers believe to be the value and observe how competitors price their products and services.

- **Take Geography into Account**

Consider the potential impact of geography on your market, if applicable. Your business plan may be impacted by regional trends, cultural preferences, and demographic differences.

.

- **Build Customer Personas**

Using the data from your research, develop thorough customer personas. These made-up depictions of your ideal clientele direct marketing initiatives and assist in customizing goods and services to meet niche demands.

- **Financial Analysis**

Evaluate the profitability of your business plan. Analyse expenses, sources of income, and possible profitability. Long-term viability depends on financial analysis.

- **Stay Ethical and Compliant**

Make sure the research you conduct complies with data protection laws and ethical standards. Observe participant privacy and make responsible use of data.

- **Iterate Based on Findings**

Utilize the new found understanding to improve your business plan. Be prepared to make adjustments in light of the feedback and information gathered throughout the investigation.

- **Seek Professional Guidance**

If your research needs specific knowledge, think about consulting with consultants or experts in market research.

Use Technology Tools

Examine the platforms and tools available in technology that make data collection and analysis easier. Data visualization platforms, analytics software, and survey tools can improve the effectiveness of your study.

- **Test Your Findings**

Prior to making important business decisions, conduct small-scale testing of your findings. To validate assumptions, this may entail limited market entry, A/B testing, or a pilot launch.

- **Monitor and Update**

Because market conditions change, you should set up a system for continuous observation. Update your research frequently to keep up with shifts in consumer preferences, market trends, and rivalry levels.

- **Embrace Continuous Learning**

Market research is a continuous undertaking. Adopt a mindset that values lifelong learning, and remain flexible in your approach to new information and shifting market conditions.

Chapter 9

Trends and Innovation

Trends and Innovation: Navigating the Evolving Business Landscape

Keeping up with trends and encouraging innovation are essential components of success in the fast-paced world of business. This is a thorough guide that will help you comprehend, take advantage of, and adjust to innovations and trends in your industry:

Understanding Trends

1. **Consumer Trends**

   - Behavioural Shifts: Track alterations in consumer behaviour, including inclinations toward internet buying, eco-friendliness, or digital experiences.
   - Demographics: Recognize how certain age groups, cultural backgrounds, or geographic areas affect consumer choices and adjust your offerings accordingly.

2. **Industry Trends**

   - Technology Integration: Examine the ways in which technology is changing your sector. Examine how these technologies, which range from blockchain to AI and IoT, can improve your goods and services.
   - Regulations: Keep abreast of any changes to the law that might have an effect on your sector in order to maintain compliance and spot business opportunities.

3. **Global Trends**

   - Globalization: Take into account how it may affect your company. Analyse the benefits and drawbacks of breaking into new markets or working with foreign partners.
   - Cultural Influences: Recognize how consumer preferences and market dynamics may be impacted by regional and global cultural trends.

Leveraging Trends

1. **Market Research**

- Constant Analysis: Keep up with market research to spot new trends and changing customer demands. Recurrent analysis keeps you on the cutting edge.
- Benchmarking your company against rivals can help you find areas where you can stand out from the crowd and take advantage of emerging trends.

2. Agile Strategies

- Adaptability: Encourage a flexible and change-embracing organizational culture. Create strategies that are flexible enough to be quickly modified in response to changing market conditions and trends.
- Pilot Initiatives: Pilot programs are a good way to test new ideas before they are implemented fully. By doing this, the risks related to unproven trends are reduced.

3. Innovation Hubs

- Establish innovation hubs inside your company to foster internal innovation. Motivate staff members to offer suggestions and cultivate an atmosphere that fosters originality.
- Collaborative Innovation: To access outside expertise and maintain your position at the forefront of innovation, work with start-up's, research institutions, or partners outside your organization.

4. Driving Innovation

- Creativity and Design Thinking: Use the concepts of design thinking to solve problems. Give priority to user-centric strategies that produce creative solutions.
- Encourage Creativity: Establish an environment in the workplace where employees are motivated to come up with new ideas and innovate.

5. Integration of Technology

- Leverage Emerging Tech: Integrate cutting-edge technologies, such as automation, machine learning, and artificial intelligence, into your business processes and product and service offerings.
- The Transition to Digital: To improve customer experiences, gain data-driven insights, and expedite procedures, think about implementing a digital transformation plan.

6. Innovation Focused on the Customer

To find out about your clients' needs and preferences, establish feedback loops with them. Utilize these comments to encourage continued development and innovation.

Co-creation of products and services should involve customers. This collaborative approach can produce solutions that truly meet the needs of the client.

7. **Adapting to Change**

- Direction and Guidance: Create a flexible, adaptable leadership style that can deal with change. Leaders need to be able to envision the company's future with clarity and inspire others to adopt change.
- At every level of the organization, promote a culture where learning never stops. It is recommended that employees upgrade their skills and adapt to industry trends.

8. **Risk Management**

- Risk assessment: Perform regular risk assessments to find possible problems associated with innovations and trends. Make plans for reducing risks in order to handle uncertainty.
- Promote the growth of a culture that honours taking calculated risks. Encourage employees to take risks, grow from their errors, and hone ideas.

9. **Networking and Collaboration**

- Engage in industry associations, forums, and networks to keep in touch with industry experts and coworkers. Cooperation can lead to opportunities and fresh viewpoints.
- Cross-Sector Cooperation: Look into collaborating with businesses outside of your industry to get fresh perspectives and insights that can inspire innovation.

10. **Measuring Success**

- Key Performance Indicators (KPIs):
- Innovation Benchmarks: Create and track metrics specific to your organization's innovation. This may include the volume of recently launched goods, the speed at which new products are created, or improvements in customer satisfaction.

11. **Market Share and Growth**

Monitor these indicators to determine how well you can capitalize on trends and innovate.

12. **Client Opinion and Contentment (Customer Feedback and Satisfaction)**

- Net Promoter Score (NPS): Measure customer satisfaction using NPS or similar metrics. Satisfied customers are more likely to be loyal and contribute to positive word-of-mouth.

13. **Employee Engagement**

- Employee Feedback: Analyse employee satisfaction and engagement levels. Engaged employees are more likely to make creative contributions and have a positive impact on the company culture.

14. **Ethical Considerations/ innovation**

- Ethical Guidelines: Establish guidelines for innovation ethics. Ensure that the way your company conducts business respects both societal norms and the privacy of your clients.
- Transparency: Be forthright and truthful about your innovative endeavours, especially if they deal with sensitive topics like data privacy or artificial intelligence.

Continuous processes of encouraging innovation and keeping a watchful eye for trends require the maintenance of a proactive and adaptable mentality. Your company can create a solid foundation for long-term success in a fast-paced business environment by understanding market dynamics, utilizing emerging trends, and cultivating an innovative culture.

Chapter 10

Creating a Business Plan

A Step-by-Step Guide to Writing a Comprehensive Business Plan

A well-structured business plan is a vital tool for managing your enterprise and attracting investors or lenders. Tailor the plan to your specific business needs, and continue to enhance it as your business grows and adapts to the needs of a shifting market.

Completing a business plan requires careful consideration and in-depth knowledge of your company, market, and industry. A well-written plan serves as your company's road map, helping you to communicate your objectives and gain the support of stakeholders.

A comprehensive business plan typically consists of several key components that provide a detailed overview of your company, including its goals, strategies, and operations. An essential tool for business owners is a well-written business plan. It provides a road map for success by outlining your company's objectives, tactics, and operational specifics.

This is a step-by-step guide to assist you in writing a thorough business plan:

1. **Executive Summary**
   - Overview: Summarize your company's goals, objectives, and the needs or problems it seeks to resolve in brief.
2. **Company Description**
   - History and Background: Give a brief overview of your company's history, mentioning its founding date and any noteworthy achievements.
   - Mission and Vision: Clearly articulate the goal and vision of your business.
   - Structure and Ownership: Describe the legal form of your business (corporation, LLC, etc.) and provide ownership details.
3. **Market Analysis**
   - Industry Overview: Provide an overview of your industry, including its current state, trends, and future outlook.
   - Identify key players and competitors in the industry.

- Market Target: Determine and characterize your target market segments' preferences, behaviours', and demographics.
- What problems and needs does your target market have that your business can help with?
- Analysis of Competition: taking note of their benefits, drawbacks, chances, and risks.
- Emphasize your unique selling points and ways to set yourself apart from the competition.
-

4. Organization and Management

- Team Overview: Introduce your management team, including key members and their roles.
- Highlight relevant experience and expertise.
- Organizational Structure: Describe your company's organizational structure.
- Clearly define reporting responsibilities and channels of contact.

5. Products and Services

- Product/Service Description: Give thorough explanations of your goods or services.
- Emphasize their special qualities.
- Development and Production: Explain the procedures used in the creation and manufacturing of your products.
- Describe any proprietary technology or intellectual property.

6. Marketing and Sales Strategy

- Market Positioning: Clearly state your value proposition to customers and your market positioning.
- Describe how you plan to position your company in the market and build brand awareness.
- Sales and Distribution Channels: Describe your distribution and sales strategies.
- Talk about how you intend to contact and assist your target clientele.

7. Marketing Plan

- Describe your marketing plans in detail, including your offline and online tactics.

- Specify your marketing channels, spending limit, and promotional initiatives.

8. Funding Request (if applicable)

- Funding Requirements: Clearly state what kind of funding you need, how much, and how you want it used.
- Describe the conditions of the financing you are requesting.
- Use of Funds: Provide a thorough budget that breaks down how the money will be distributed.
- Financial Projections: Give an explanation for every expense and how it affects your company.
- Revenue Forecast: Provide a thorough revenue forecast that includes sales estimates for the ensuing three to five years.
- Include the factors and assumptions that will affect your projections.
- Expense Budget: Describe your spending plan in detail, including expenses for staff, operations, and marketing.
- Give a detailed breakdown of your fixed and variable costs.
- Cash Flow Statement: Give a cash flow statement that shows the inflow and outflow of funds from your company.
- Emphasize times when cash flow was both positive and negative.

9. Risk Analysis

- Identify Risks: Determine the risks and difficulties that your company might encounter.
- Evaluate each risk's likelihood and possible consequences.
- Risk Mitigation: Describe methods for reducing hazards that have been identified.
- Describe backup plans and how you'll handle unforeseen difficulties.

10. Implementation Plan

- Timeline: Establish a schedule for carrying out important tasks and benchmarks.
- Divide the plan into doable sections.
- Responsibilities: Assign duties to each project or achievement.
- Clearly state who is responsible for each plan element's successful execution.

11. Monitoring and Evaluation

- Key Performance Indicators (KPIs): Establish KPIs that are consistent with your company's objectives.
- Create metrics to gauge the level of achievement.
- Monitoring and Review: Describe a procedure for routine observation and evaluation.
- Indicate how frequently you will review the plan's progress and make changes.

12. Appendices and Supporting Documents

- Additional Information: Provide any extra data that bolsters your business plan. Include pertinent documents, such as legal documents, resumes, and data from market research.

Last but not least, ensure that your business plan is focused, clear, and concise. Avoid using unnecessary or overly complicated jargon.

- Maintain a realistic perspective in your estimations and evaluations. Stakeholders and investors value honesty and reasonable expectations.
- Update it frequently to reflect changes in your industry, market conditions, or business strategies. View your business plan as a living document that changes as your company does
- Modify and improve your strategy in response to new information, market developments, and feedback.
- Use visual aids like tables, graphs, and charts to improve comprehension. • Complex information can be communicated more successfully when presented visually.
- To get feedback, show your business plan to dependable advisors, industry experts, or mentors.
- Seek constructive feedback to improve the standard and effectiveness of your plan.

Chapter 11

<u>Setting Goals and Objectives</u>

The process of creating measurable, clear goals and objectives is a crucial component of strategic planning for any project or company. Even though goals provide direction, objectives are the specific, attainable steps that lead to achieving goals. This guide will help you set and achieve realistic goals and objectives:

Setting Goals

1. **Define Your Vision**
   - To begin, clearly and succinctly state the overall goal of your project or company.
   - Which long-term objectives are you thinking of?
2. **Identify Key Focus Areas**
   - Break the vision up into main points of emphasis or themes. These could be linked to growth, innovation, customer satisfaction, or other strategic priorities.
3. **Make Goals SMART**
   - Ensure your goals are SMART: Specific, Measurable, Achievable, Relevant, and Time-bound. This framework makes goals clear and actionable.
   - Specific: Clearly state what must be accomplished.
   - Measurable: Create metrics to monitor success and progress.
   - Achievable: Establish attainable and realistic goals.
   - Relevant: Align goals with your overall vision and strategy.
   - Time-bound: Specify a timeframe for achieving each goal.
4. **Prioritize Goals**
   - Prioritize and rank your objectives according to how they will affect your overall vision. This makes it easier to focus efforts on the most important tasks.
   - Consider Long-Term and Short-Term Goals:

   -

- Understand the distinctions between short-term (tactical) and long-term (strategic) goals. Long-term goals establish the direction, whereas short-term goals aid in the immediate progress.

5. Align with Values and Mission

- Verify that your objectives line up with your company's mission and values. This kind of alignment encourages a methodical and purposeful approach.

<u>**Setting Objectives**</u>

1. Break Down Goals into Objectives

- Divide each goal into a set of focused objectives. The specific actions that lead to the accomplishment of the overarching goal are known as objectives.

2. Specify Actions and Tasks

- Clearly outline the steps and duties needed to complete each goal. This offers an implementation road map.

3. Quantify Where Possible

- By allocating precise metrics or key performance indicators (KPIs), make goals quantifiable. Tracking progress becomes more concrete when objectives are quantified.

4. Assign Responsibilities

- Clearly designate who is responsible for each goal. Indicate who will be responsible for seeing that the tasks related to the goal are completed successfully.

5. Establish a Timeline

- Establish a deadline for finishing each goal. This ensures an organized implementation process and aids in fostering a sense of urgency.

6. Verify Alignment

- This involves making sure that every goal has a direct relationship to each of the objectives. This alignment guarantees that attaining objectives adds to the company's overall success.

7. Review and Adjust Frequently

- Evaluate goals' progress on a regular basis. As circumstances, the market, or internal factors change, objectives should be adjusted as necessary.

8. Track and Recognize Success

- Create a framework for tracking advancement and acknowledging successes. Acknowledging accomplishments inspires groups and keeps the momentum going
- Adapt to Change
- Be adaptable and willing to change plans and goals in response to criticism, changes in the market, or unforeseen difficulties.

The process of establishing goals and objectives must be reviewed and adjusted on a regular basis. You can give your company a successful roadmap and guarantee that it stays focused on its strategic priorities by establishing a well-organized framework and matching specific goals with overarching objectives.

Chapter 12

Regulatory and Legal Aspects

Legal and regulatory matters must be carefully considered before beginning and operating a business. For your business to run smoothly and morally, you have to abide by all applicable laws and regulations.

Please review the following guide to help you navigate legal and regulatory matters:

1. **Structure of Organizations**
    - Select the Appropriate Legal Framework
    - Decide whether your company will be run as a corporation, LLC, partnership, or sole proprietorship. The legal ramifications for governance, taxation, and liability vary depending on the structure
    - Register Your Business
    - Officially register your business with the relevant government agencies. This usually entails registering the company name and obtaining a business license.

2. **Permits and Licenses for Businesses**
    - Research Local Regulations
    - Determine which licenses and permits—local, state, and federal—are specific to your type of business. Conditions vary by industry and geographic location.
    - Obtain the required permits before starting operations. Environmental, zoning, health, and other permits could be among them.

3. **Employment Laws**
    - Recognize the Employment Rules
    - Learn about labour laws, including those that deal with minimum wage requirements, working hours, overtime pay, and benefits for employees.
    - Provisional Employment Contracts: Draft comprehensive and unambiguous employment contracts that specify all relevant terms and conditions of employment, such as duties, pay, and procedures for termination.

4. **Protection of Intellectual Property (IP)**

- Identify and Protect Intellectual Property: List any intellectual property (IP) that your company owns, including patents, copyrights, and trademarks. Ensure that these assets are registered and protected.
- NDAs, or non-disclosure agreements: To safeguard sensitive data, use non-disclosure agreements when disclosing private information to contractors, employees, or business partners.

5. **Contractual Agreements**

- Draft clear contracts for joint ventures, business transactions, and collaborations. Clearly state the conditions, deliverables, terms of payment, and procedures for resolving disputes.
- Review and Negotiate Contracts: Examine contracts carefully before signing. If required, get legal counsel to make sure you comprehend the terms and engage in any necessary negotiations.

6. **Tax Requirements**

- Recognize Tax Obligations: Adhere to federal, state, and local tax regulations. Recognize the income tax, sales tax, and employment tax obligations that apply to your company.
- Maintain Accurate Financial Record Keep accurate financial records to ensure tax compliance. To ensure accuracy, consider hiring a professional accountant.

7. **Data security and privacy**

- Obey Data Protection Laws: If your business gathers and uses personal data, adhere to privacy and data protection regulations. Take the California Consumer Privacy Act (CCPA) or the General Data Protection Regulation (GDPR) regulations, for example.
- Put in Place Security Measures: Install cybersecurity safeguards to protect customer and employee information. This covers encryption, safe storage, and routine evaluations of data security.

8. **Environmental and Safety Regulations**

- Adhere to Environmental Standards: Comply with environmental regulations if your business operations have an impact on the environment. This could include waste disposal, emissions control, and environmental practices.
- Ensure Workplace Safety: Create and implement safety procedures to guarantee a secure workplace for staff members. Respect the guidelines set forth by the Occupational Safety and Health Administration (OSHA).

9. Accessibility Compliance

- Ensure Accessibility: To accommodate people with disabilities, make sure your company complies with accessibility standards, especially for online platforms.

10. Consumer Protection Laws

- Know Consumer Rights: Understand consumer protection laws that apply to your industry. Clearly communicate product/service warranties, refund policies, and terms of sale.
- Handle Customer Data Responsibly: To preserve customer privacy, if your company gathers customer data, use responsible data handling procedures.

11. Legal Counsel

Seek Legal Advice: Consult with legal professionals for guidance on complex legal matters. An attorney specializing in business law can provide valuable advice and ensure compliance.

Final Tips:

- Stay Informed: Regularly update yourself on changes in laws and regulations relevant to your industry. Legal requirements can evolve, and staying informed is crucial for compliance.
- Documentation: Keep thorough documentation of compliance efforts. This includes contracts, permits, licenses, and any communication related to legal matters.
- Ethical Conduct: Conduct your business ethically. While legal compliance is essential, ethical practices contribute to a positive reputation and long-term success.

For businesses, navigating legal and regulatory issues is a continuous process. Maintaining awareness, getting legal counsel when necessary, and taking proactive measures to handle compliance issues can help you lay the groundwork for a profitable and compliant business enterprise.

Chapter 13

Business Structures

Choosing the right business structure is crucial because it influences your company's governance, taxes, and liability, among other things. Here are some examples of common business structures, each with special characteristics:

1. **Sole Proprietorship**
   - Description: Run and owned by a solitary person
   - Simplest and most common form of business structure.

Key Characteristics:

- Total control and power to make decisions.
- Under pass-through taxation, profits and losses are reported on the owner's personal tax return; Individual accountability for business debts.
- Suitable for small businesses with low regulatory requirements, it should be taken into consideration.
- Limited capacity for capital raising.

2. **Partnership**
   - Description: Business owned by two or more individuals.

Key Characteristics:

- Decentralized control and decision-making.
- Personal liability for commercial debts.
- Taxation at the source.

Considerations:

- General Partnerships: All partners share equally in management and liability.
- Limited Partnerships: Limited partners have lower liability but less control.

3. **Limited Liability Company (LLC)**
   - Description: Hybrid structure combining features of a corporation and partnership.

- **Key Characteristics**
- Owners' (members') liability is limited.
- Management structure that is adaptable.
- Taxation at the source.
- **Considerations:**
- Suitable for small to medium-sized businesses.
- Offers personal asset protection.

4. **Corporation**
   - Description: Legal entity separates from its owners (shareholders).
   - **Key Characteristics:**
   - Limited liability for shareholders.
   - Centralized management with a board of directors.
   - Double taxation (corporate and individual taxes on profits).
   - **Considerations:**
   - C-corporation: Standard corporation with potential for many shareholders.
   - S-corporation: Allows pass-through taxation, limited to 100 shareholders.

5. **Non-profit Corporation:**
   - Description: Formed for charitable, educational, religious, or other non-profit purposes.
   - **Key Characteristics:**
   - Exempt from certain taxes.
   - Limited ability to distribute profits to individuals.
   - Governed by a board of directors.
   - **Considerations:**
   - Must meet specific criteria to maintain non-profit status.
   - Focus on fulfilling a mission rather than generating profit.

6. **Cooperative:**
   - Description: Owned and operated by its members for mutual benefit.
   - **Key Characteristics:**
   - Members actively participate in decision-making.
   - Profits shared among members.

- **Considerations:**
- Often formed to meet common needs or goals of members.
- Examples include agricultural cooperatives or consumer cooperatives.

7. **Professional Corporation:**
   - Description: Formed by licensed professionals (e.g., doctors, lawyers, accountants).
   - Crucial Features: Restricted accountability for errors made by professionals.
   - Members need to hold the appropriate professional license.
   - **Considerations:**
   - Protects professionals who work for the company against personal liability.

Things to Take into Account While Selecting a Business Structure

- **Liability:** Think about how much personal liability coverage you actually require. Partnerships and sole proprietorships provide less protection than corporations and LLCs.
  - **Tax Implications:** Understand how your taxes are impacted by each structure. Pass-through taxation is a common feature of S-corporations, LLCs, partnerships, and sole proprietorships.
  - **Management and Control**: Arrange your ideas regarding the company's management. Some organizational structures, like corporations, have a more centralized management structure.
  - **Complexity and Regulation**: Define the legal and administrative requirements for each structure. Generally speaking, partnerships and sole proprietorships need less paperwork than corporations do.
  - **Capital and Funding:** Consider how you intend to raise capital. Corporations have the advantage of attracting investors by issuing stock.
  - **Future Growth:** Analyse your long-term growth strategies. As your business expands, some structures might be more scalable and flexible.

Getting advice from legal and financial experts is a good idea when choosing the best business structure for your unique situation. Every structure has benefits and drawbacks, and the best option will rely on your company's objectives, the state of the market, and applicable laws.

Chapter 14

Intellectual Property

The term "intellectual property" (IP) describes any works of literature, art, inventions, designs, names, symbols, and pictures that are used in trade. Patents, copyrights, trademarks, and trade secrets are examples of intellectual property that are legally protected and give creators and owners the ability to govern and profit from their creations.

The primary forms of intellectual property and their respective methods of protection are as follows:

1. **Patents:**
   - Purpose: Preserves discoveries and inventions.
   - Requirements: Needs to be new, obscure, and practical.
   - Protection: Gives the creator of the invention the only authority to produce, use, and market the invention for a set amount of time—typically 20 years.

2. **Copyright:**
   - Purpose: Protects original works of authorship.
   - Coverage: Relates to artistic, musical, literary, and other creative works.
   - Protection: The author is given the sole authority to copy, distribute, perform, and exhibit the work. Protection usually extends for the author's lifetime plus an additional seventy years.

3. **Trademarks:**
   - Goal: Safeguards names, symbols, catchphrases, and other identifiers applied to products or services.
   - Security: Gives the trademark owner the only authority to use it in commercial endeavours. For as long as the mark is being used, protection can be extended indefinitely.

4. **Trade Secrets:**

- Purpose: Protects confidential business information.
- Coverage: Consists of any information, such as formulas, processes, designs, patterns, or other data, that provides a business advantage.
- Protection: Insists on the information's confidentiality. Protection will continue so long as the data is kept private.

5. **Trade Dress:**
   - Purpose: Protects the visual appearance and overall impression of a product.
   - Coverage: Includes the design and packaging of a product.
   - Protection: Protecting against consumer confusion, akin to trademark protection.

6. **Industrial Design Rights**:
   - Purpose: Preserves an object's aesthetic appeal.
   - Coverage: Concerns an object's visual qualities.
   - Protection: The owner is granted exclusive rights for a specific duration.

7. **Plant Variety Protection:**
   - Purpose: Protects new varieties of plants.
   - Coverage: Concerns plants propagated by tubercles or sexual reproduction.
   - Protection: Grants the owner exclusive rights to market the new plant variety for a specified period.

Key Considerations of intellectual property

1. **Registration**: It is necessary to register certain types of intellectual property, like patents, trademarks, and copyrights, with the appropriate government offices in order to obtain legal protection.
2. **Enforcement:** The owner of intellectual property must actively defend their rights. Legal action against those who violate the protected rights may be necessary in this situation.
3. **Licensing:** Intellectual property owners can grant licenses to third parties so they can use their works in exchange for payments or royalties.

4. **International Protection**: The protection of intellectual property is territorial. If your company conducts business abroad, you might want to think about obtaining protection in several jurisdictions.
5. **Due Diligence:** Make sure intellectual property doesn't violate any existing rights before adopting or using it. In a similar vein, make sure your intellectual property is new and protected by conducting searches.

Enforcement Mechanisms of intellectual property

1. **Cease and Desist Letters**: Inform alleged infringers of the violation and demand that they stop the infringing activity.
2. **Litigation:** Legal action can be taken to enforce intellectual property rights and seek damages for infringement.
3. **Alternative Dispute Resolution:** Mediation or arbitration can be used as alternatives to litigation for resolving intellectual property disputes.

•   Maintaining a competitive edge and assuring the long-term viability of your company depend heavily on your ability to comprehend and safeguard your intellectual property. Seeking advice from legal experts in intellectual property law can help you determine the most effective methods for safeguarding your works.

Compliance and Regulations

Businesses must abide by laws and regulations in order to conduct themselves morally, sustainably, and within the bounds of the law. Different facets of business operations are governed by a variety of laws and regulations.

These are the main regulatory and compliance areas that businesses frequently need to take into account.:

1. **Business Registration and Licensing**:
•   Business Structure: Decide on the best legal form for your company (corporation, LLC, sole proprietorship, etc.) and register it appropriately.

- Local, State, and Federal Licenses: Depending on your industry and location, get the required licenses and permits at the local, state, and federal levels.

2. **Employment Laws:**

- Overtime and Minimum Wage: Adhere to the rules regarding overtime and minimum wage. Make sure workers receive just compensation.
- Laws that Prohibit Discrimination: Comply with anti-discrimination laws to advance fair treatment of workers and equal employment opportunities.
- Workplace Safety: To keep your workplace safe, abide by Occupational Safety and Health Administration (OSHA) regulations.

3. **Rules Regarding Taxes:**

- Income Tax: Be aware of and compliant with local, state, and federal income tax laws.
- Sales Tax: Collect and file sales tax on applicable goods and services in accordance with local laws.
- Taxes on Employment: Payroll taxes ought to be withheld and remitted, along with Social Security and Medicare contributions.

4. **Privacy and Data Protection**:

  - Personal Information: Comply with privacy and data protection laws to protect the personal information of clients and employees.
  - Notification Conditions: Report the information in accordance with the guidelines in the event of a security breach.

5. **Guidelines for the Environment:**

- Waste Disposal: Get rid of waste in accordance with environmental laws.
- Emissions Control: Comply with laws governing emissions and pollutants, particularly for sectors of the economy that have an influence on the environment.

6. **Rights to Intellectual Property:**

- Copyrights, trademarks, and patents: Honour and defend the rights to intellectual property. Make certain that your company does not violate the patents, trademarks, or copyrights of others.

7. **Laws Protecting Consumers:**

- Sincerity in Promotion: Comply with regulations pertaining to truth in advertising, guaranteeing truthful and open communication with customers.

- Product Safety: Adhere to laws governing the labelling and safety of products.

8. Competition and Antitrust Laws:

- Collusion and Price Fixation: Steer clear of actions like price-fixing and collusion that are prohibited by antitrust laws.
- Fair Competition: Encourage fair competition and abstain from anti-competitive actions.

9. Financial Regulations:

- Standards for Accounting: Adhere to accounting guidelines to guarantee precise financial reporting.
- Laws that prevent money laundering (AML): Adhere to AML regulations by putting in place measures to identify and stop money laundering.

10. Regulations for Health and Safety:

- Industry-Specific Regulations: Comply with industry-specific safety and health requirements. The food industry, for instance, might have particular requirements for hygiene.
- Employee Health and Safety: Establish a secure workplace and follow all applicable laws pertaining to workers' health and safety.

11. Contractual Agreements:

- Adherence to Consent: Check to see that the terms and conditions included in agreements with vendors, partners, and suppliers are being adhered to.
- Protocols for Execution: Programs to Promote Internal Compliance:

Establish internal compliance initiatives to ensure that employees understand and abide by relevant laws and regulations.

12. Assessments and Audits:

- Regularly identify and assess non-compliance areas by conducting audits and assessments.
- Legal Advice: To guarantee adherence to constantly changing laws and handle intricate regulations, consult a lawyer.
- Stay informed about any modifications to the laws and rules that may impact your business.

- Be ready to modify company procedures in reaction to modifications in regulations.
- Employees should receive continual training to make sure they understand the requirements for compliance.

Apart from being mandated by law, upholding adherence to laws and regulations is crucial to gaining the confidence of relevant parties like investors, consumers, and other concerned parties. Adapting your compliance efforts to the ever-changing regulatory landscape requires ongoing evaluation and revision. Seeking guidance from industry experts and legal counsel can provide crucial direction for maintaining a compliant business operation.

Chapter 15

<u>Funding Your Venture</u>

Funding is an important part of starting and growing a business. There are numerous funding options, each with its own set of benefits and drawbacks. Here are some common methods for funding your venture:

- Starting from scratch
- Friends and Family
- Angel Investors
- Venture Capital (VC)
- Crowdfunding
- Bank Loans
- Small Business Grants
- Corporate Partnerships
- Government Loans and Programs
- Strategic Investors:

<u>Key Considerations for Funding Your Venture</u>

1. **Business Plan**: Create a detailed business plan that outlines your business model, market, and financial projections.
2. **Pitch:** Make a compelling pitch in order to attract investors. Communicate your venture's value proposition and growth potential clearly.
3. **Due Diligence:** Prepare to provide precise and detailed information about your company. Investors will conduct due diligence. Be prepared to provide accurate and detailed information about your business.
4. **Legal and Financial Advisors:** To navigate funding agreements and ensure compliance, consult with legal and financial advisors.

5. **Valuation:** Determine a reasonable valuation for your company. Be prepared to bargain with investors.
6. **Use of Funds:** Explain how the funds will be used and the anticipated impact on the business.

- Diversification: Consider diversifying your funding sources to reduce reliance on a single type of funding.

Your company's stage, industry, and growth objectives will determine which funding source is best for it. It is essential to carefully weigh the terms and ramifications of each funding option and, if needed, to consult a professional. Fundraising can also be aided by establishing a solid network and fostering relationships with potential investors.

Chapter 16

Building a Strong Team

Creating a solid and productive team is crucial to any company's success. A motivated and cohesive team can boost overall business performance, productivity, and innovation. The following are crucial methods for creating a powerful team:

1. **Clearly Specify Your Duties and Roles**:

- Job Descriptions: Clearly outline the roles and responsibilities of each team member through well-defined job descriptions.
- Expectations: Establish clear guidelines for both team and individual performance. Set quantifiable objectives and targets.

2. **Recruit and Select Talent Thoughtfully:**

- Skills and Qualifications: Determine the abilities and credentials required for each position. Seek applicants whose abilities complement the team environment as well as the job specifications.
- Cultural Fit: Take prospective team members' cultural fit into consideration. Common values and working styles are frequently shared by a cohesive team.
- Diverse Perspectives: Assemble a group of people with varying experiences and viewpoints. Diverse teams can contribute originality and various approaches to problem-solving.

3. **Promote Effective Communication:**

- Open Dialogue: Encourage candid dialogue among team members. Encourage team members to voice their opinions and concerns in a relaxed atmosphere.

- Feedback: Encourage a culture of constructive criticism and give regular feedback. Constructive criticism encourages growth, whereas positive criticism highlights excellent performance.
- Meetings with the team: Call frequent team meetings to go over goals, projects, and any difficulties. These gatherings keep everyone informed and on the same page.

4. **Promote an Upbeat Workplace Culture**:

- The company's mission and values should be communicated in an understandable manner. Ensure that each member of the team understands and is dedicated to these core principles.

5. **Recognize and Celebrate Achievements**:

- Recognize and celebrate both large and small achievements. Recognizing individual and team accomplishments boosts morale.
- Inclusivity: Create an inclusive environment in which all team members feel valued and included. Avoid favouritism and promote cooperation.

6. **Make Opportunities for Skill Development Available**

- Training Courses: Invest in training programs to improve team members' skills and knowledge. This can help with both individual development and team performance.
- Mentoring: Establish mentorship programs within the team. Experienced team members can guide and support those who are newer or less experienced.

7. **Empower and Delegate**

- Delegate responsibilities based on individual strengths. Empower team members by entrusting them with meaningful tasks.
- Autonomy: Allow team members some degree of autonomy in decision-making. This fosters a sense of ownership and responsibility.

8. **Build Trust and Collaboration**

- Transparency: Be transparent with information and decisions. Building trust requires open communication and honesty.
- Team-Building Activities: Organize team-building activities to strengthen relationships and improve collaboration. This can include both work-related and social events.

9. **Handle Conflict Constructively**:
   - Conflict Resolution: Address conflicts promptly and constructively. Establish a process for resolving disagreements and encourage open dialogue to find solutions.
   - Mediation: When necessary, involve a neutral mediator to help facilitate conflict resolution discussions.

10. **Promote Work-Life Balance**

- Flexible Work Arrangements: When it's feasible, provide flexible work schedules. Encouraging work-life balance enhances job satisfaction and employee well-being.
- Respect Personal Time: Observe personal space and schedules. Refrain from expecting to be available at all times outside of regular business hours.

11. **Lead by Example**

- Leadership Integrity: Set an example of integrity in leadership and conduct that you would like to see from your team. Setting a good example for the rest of the organization is important.
- Adaptability: Show adaptability and resilience in the face of challenges. Your response to adversity can influence the team's morale and approach to problem-solving.

Developing a strong team is a continuous process that calls for consideration of each team member's unique needs as well as the dynamics of the group. Evaluate team performance on a regular basis, get input, and adjust as necessary. You can build a team that not only succeeds in achieving its objectives but also thrives and takes pleasure in the journey as a whole by cultivating a positive and cooperative environment.

Chapter 17

Marketing and Branding

Branding and marketing are essential to any company's success. Robust brands foster both confidence and loyalty, while effective marketing spreads the word, draws in clients, and increases sales.

The following are crucial branding and marketing tactics:

Techniques for Promotion

1. **Choose the Identity of Your Target Market**:

• **Customer Persona**: Develop thorough customer personas to discover more about the traits, proclivities, and behaviours of your target audience.

• **Market segmentation**: To focus your marketing efforts, divide your market into smaller groups according to common needs.

2. **Create a Sturdy Online Presence**

•Web-based platform: Create a visually appealing and easy-to-use website. Make sure it includes a call to action that is obvious and details about your goods or services.

3. **Social Networks**
- Make use of the social media sites where people in your target market are active. Share thought-provoking content on a regular basis to keep your audience engaged.
- Providing your target audience with engaging, informative, or thought-provoking blog posts, videos, or infographics is known as content marketing.

4. **Make Use of SEO (Search Engine Optimization)**
- Keyword optimization: Make sure your website's content and keywords are optimized to improve its position in search results.

- Excellent content: Give your audience relevant, high-quality content that is customized to meet their needs.
- Paid Advertising: Google Ads: Target particular keywords with Google Ads to show up in search results.
- Social media marketing: To reach your audience, place targeted advertisements on websites like Facebook, Instagram, LinkedIn, and others.

5. **Email marketing**
   - Compile and organize email addresses so that each recipient receives a customized message. Make an e-mail database.
   - Robotics: Use email automation to interact with customers.
   - Partnerships: Establish alliances with influencers or other companies that share your values.

Strategies for Branding:

1. **Establish Your Unique Brand**

• Goals and Principles: Clearly state the goals and core principles of your business. Share these components in a consistent manner.

• Personality of Brand: Describe the character of your brand. Is it amiable, competent, creative, or daring?

2. **Design an Iconic Visual Identity and Logo**
   - Logo Design: Create a unique, memorable logo that captures the essence of your company.
   - Colour Scheme and Font: Choose a colour scheme and font that work well together to be used in all branding materials.

3. **Steady Brand Communication**
   - Tagline: Craft a succinct and unforgettable tagline that captures the essence of your brand.
   - Voice and Tone: Whether speaking or writing, always have a consistent voice and tone.

4. **Customer Experience**
   - Customer Service: Offer superior customer service to establish favourable connotations with your brand.

- The goal of user experience (UX) is to guarantee a smooth and enjoyable online and offline user experience.

5. **Narration:**

- Brand Story: Ensure that your brand tells an engaging story that emotionally engages your target audience.
- Case Studies: Distribute case studies and success stories that demonstrate how your goods or services have benefited people.

6. **Observe and Modify:**

- Brand Assessments: Perform periodic brand audits to evaluate the market performance of your brand.
- **Customer feedback:** To determine areas that require improvement, gather and examine customer feedback.

7. **Social Responsibility and Community Engagement**:

- Take part in social responsibility programs that complement your brand's core values.
- Community Building: Organize events, social media groups, or online forums to create a community around your brand.

8. **Calculate Brand Equity**

- Feedback and Surveys: Measure brand perception, loyalty, and awareness through feedback and surveys.
- Analytics: Keep an eye on online sentiment and engagement by utilizing analytics tools.

9. **Adjust for Trends in the Market**

- Keep up with market developments and modify your branding tactics as necessary.
- Originality: To remain competitive, embrace innovation in branding and marketing.

10. **Brand Advocacy by Employees:**

- Educating: Instruct employees on how to embody the Long-term business success requires integrating strong brand identity with effective marketing strategies.

- One way to establish a strong and recognizable brand in the market is to know who your target audience is, use a variety of marketing channels, and reinforce your brand values frequently.
- To remain current and resonate with your audience, review and modify your strategies on a regular basis.

Chapter 18

<u>Scaling Your Business</u>

Scaling a business is a complex process that requires a comprehensive and well-executed strategy. It involves aligning various aspects of the business, including operations, finances, marketing, and human resources, to support increased demand and reach new markets.

Regularly assess your progress, adapt strategies as needed, and remain agile to navigate the challenges associated with growth. Successful scaling positions your business for long-term success and sustainability

Scaling a business involves increasing its size and capacity to handle a higher volume of operations, customers, and market demands. Successful scaling requires careful planning, resource management, and strategic decision-making.

Here are key strategies for scaling your business:

1. **Clear Growth Strategy**:
- Define Objectives: Clearly define your growth objectives. Are you expanding into new markets, increasing production, or launching new products/services?
- Market Analysis: Conduct a thorough market analysis to identify growth opportunities and potential challenges.

2. **Optimize Operations**:
- Streamline Processes: Identify and streamline operational processes to improve efficiency. Eliminate bottlenecks and unnecessary steps.
- Technology Integration: Integrate technology solutions to automate repetitive tasks and enhance productivity.

3. **Financial Planning:**
- Capital Allocation: Allocate resources strategically. Ensure that funding is allocated to areas that directly contribute to growth.

- Cash Flow Management: During the scaling process, effectively manage cash flow to support increased operational demands.

4. **Talent Development and Acquisition**:
   - Recruiting Approach: Formulate a strong recruiting approach in order to draw in top candidates. As the workload increases, scale your team accordingly.
   - Training Programs: • Establish training initiatives to give staff members the tools they need to take on more responsibility.

5. **Technology Investment:**
   - Scalable Systems: Invest in scalable systems that can accommodate higher volumes without experiencing appreciable cost increases.
   - Data Analytics: Make use of data analytics to learn about market trends, consumer behaviour, and operational effectiveness.

6. **Customer Acquisition and Retention**

- Marketing Campaigns: Develop targeted marketing campaigns to reach new customers and markets.
- Customer Retention Programs: Implement customer retention programs to ensure existing customers remain satisfied and loyal.

7. **Supply Chain Optimization:**

- Supplier Relationships: Strengthen relationships with suppliers to ensure a stable and efficient supply chain.
- Inventory Management: Optimize inventory management to meet increased demand without excess or shortage.

8. **Expand Product/Service Offerings**:

- Product Diversification: Expand your product or service offerings to cater to a broader customer base.
- Market Testing: Test new products or services in the market before full-scale implementation.

9. **Geographical Expansion:**

- New Markets: Explore opportunities for geographical expansion into new regions or countries.
- Localized Marketing: Tailor marketing strategies to specific regions to resonate with local audiences.

   10. Strategic Partnerships:

- Collaborate with Key Partners: Form strategic partnerships that can provide
  support, resources, or access to new markets.
- Joint Ventures: Consider joint ventures with other businesses to share risks
  and resources.

   11. Customer Feedback and Iteration:

- Continuous Improvement: Continuously gather customer feedback and iterate
  on your products, services, and processes.
- Agile Approach: Embrace an agile approach to respond quickly to changing
  market conditions and customer needs.

   12. Risk Management:

- Identify and Mitigate Risks: Conduct risk assessments to identify potential
  challenges. Develop strategies to mitigate risks associated with scaling.
- Scenario Planning: Plan for various scenarios to ensure resilience in the face
  of unforeseen challenges.

13. Maintain Company Culture:

- Cultural Alignment: Ensure that the company culture is aligned with growth
  objectives. Communicate the values and vision that guide the organization.
- Employee Engagement: Foster a positive and engaged workforce to maintain
  a collaborative and innovative environment.

14. Legal and Regulatory Compliance:

- Compliance Management: Stay informed about legal and regulatory
  requirements in new markets. Ensure compliance with local laws.
- Risk of Expansion: Assess and manage the legal and regulatory risks
  associated with business expansion.

15. Monitoring and Evaluation:

- Key Performance Indicators (KPIs): Establish KPIs to measure the success of
  your scaling efforts. Regularly monitor and evaluate performance against
  these metrics.
- **Feedback Loops**: Implement feedback loops to capture insights from
  employees, customers, and stakeholders.

<u>Techniques for Expanding/ Strategies for Growth</u>

Business growth strategies are necessary to maintain and increase a company's market share. Growth strategies can take many different forms, such as expanding into new markets or offering already-existing products and services.

Innovation, adaptability, and strategic planning are all necessary for successful business growth. To improve and modify growth strategies, it is essential to routinely assess internal capabilities, customer feedback, and market conditions. A combination of these tactics, each adapted to the particular traits and objectives of your company, is frequently necessary for successful expansion.

The following are important tactics to attain business growth:

1. **Market Penetration:**
   - Sell More to Current Clients: Motivate Current Clients to Purchase More by Introducing Loyalty Programs, Upselling, or Complementary Products.
   - Acquire a Greater Market Share: Pay attention to expanding your market share by surpassing rivals or reaching unexplored clientele.
2. **Product Development:**
   - Broaden your product/service offerings to satisfy changing client needs. • Introduce New Products or Services. This could entail improvements, modifications, or brand-new products.
   - Innovation: To maintain your innovativeness, spend money on research and development. Present innovative features•
3. **Enter New Markets:**
   - Explore new geographical locations or demographics. Consider international expansion or targeting different customer segments.
   - Diversification: Diversify into new markets that may be related or unrelated to your current offerings. This can mitigate risks and open new revenue streams.
4. **Strategic Partnerships and Alliances:**
   - Collaborate with Other Businesses: Form partnerships or alliances with other businesses to leverage each other's strengths and resources.

- Joint Ventures: Consider joint ventures where two or more companies collaborate on a specific project or venture

5. **Merger and Acquisition:**

- Acquire Other Businesses: Acquire companies that complement your business, provide access to new markets, or enhance your capabilities.
- Merger: Consider merging with another company to create synergies and strengthen your market position.
- Franchising: Expand your business by offering franchise opportunities. This allows others to replicate your successful business model under your brand.
- License your brand, products, or services to others for use in specific markets or industries.

6. **E-commerce and Digital Expansion**:

- Online Presence: Strengthen your online presence. Invest in e-commerce capabilities and digital marketing to reach a wider audience.
- Digital Products or Services: Explore opportunities to offer digital products or services that can be delivered online.

7. **Customer Retention:**

- Focus on Customer Loyalty: Implement strategies to enhance customer satisfaction and loyalty. Loyal customers are more likely to make repeat purchases and recommend your business.
- Customer Relationship Management (CRM): Utilize CRM systems to manage and analyse customer interactions, improving communication and service.

8. **Operational Efficiency:**

- Streamline Operations: Identify and eliminate inefficiencies in your operations. This can improve productivity and reduce costs.
- Supply Chain Optimization: Optimize your supply chain to enhance efficiency and responsiveness to market demands.

9. **Employee Training and Development:**

- Invest in Talent: Provide training and development opportunities for your employees to enhance their skills. A skilled workforce contributes to organizational growth.
- **Employee Engagement**: Foster a positive work culture that encourages employee engagement and retention.

10. **Customer Feedback and Data Analytics**:

- Data-Driven Decision-Making: Use customer feedback and data analytics to make informed business decisions. Understand market trends and customer preferences.
- Continuous Improvement: Continuously analyse and improve your products, services, and processes based on feedback and data.

11. **Financial Management:**

- Capital Management: Manage capital effectively to support growth initiatives. This may involve securing financing, managing cash flow, and optimizing financial resources.
- Risk Management: Mitigate financial risks by conducting thorough risk assessments and implementing risk management strategies.

13. **Sustainability and Corporate Social Responsibility (CSR):**

- Sustainable Practices: Embrace sustainable and socially responsible practices. Consumers increasingly value businesses that prioritize environmental and social responsibility.
- CSR Initiatives: Engage in CSR initiatives that align with your brand values and resonate with customers.

12. **Agile and Adaptive Leadership**:

- Adaptability: Foster a culture of adaptability and innovation. Leaders should be open to change and encourage a dynamic and responsive organization.
- Agile Methodology: Implement agile methodologies to quickly respond to market changes and customer needs.

13. **Customer-Centric Approach:**

- Personalization: Personalize your products, services, and marketing strategies based on individual customer preferences.
- User Experience (UX): To increase client loyalty and satisfaction, give top priority to a good user experience.

Managing Expansion

Overseeing growth is an essential stage in a company's development process. A smooth and successful transition to a larger scale requires strategic planning, effective leadership, and efficient resource allocation.

Managing expansion is a complex and dynamic process that requires careful planning, adaptability, and effective execution. By addressing key considerations in areas such as finance, talent, technology, and customer experience, you can navigate the challenges of expansion and position your business for sustained growth. Regularly assess your strategies, learn from experiences, and continuously improve to ensure the success of the expansion process.

Important considerations and strategies for managing growth include the following:

1. **Planning Strategically**

• **Clearly Stated Goals**: Clearly state what the expansion's goals are. Recognize the precise objectives you hope to accomplish, such as expanding your product line, breaking into untapped markets, or raising production levels.

• **Market Research**: Identify opportunities and challenges in the new markets or sectors you plan to enter by conducting in-depth market research.

2. **Financial Management**:
   - Budgeting: Create a detailed budget that addresses every facet of the growth, such as operations, technology, marketing, and hiring new staff.
   - Financial Modelling: Apply financial modelling techniques to evaluate

3. **Recruitment Strategy**:
   - Develop a robust recruitment strategy to attract and onboard new talent. Ensure that your team has the skills and expertise needed for the expanded operations.
   - Training Programs: Implement training programs to equip existing employees with the skills required for their evolving roles.

4. **Technology Integration**:

- Scalable Systems: Invest in scalable technology systems that can handle the increased workload. Ensure that your IT infrastructure can support the expanded operations.
- Data Security: Implement robust cybersecurity measures to protect sensitive data as your business grows.

5. Operational Efficiency:

- Process Optimization: Continuously optimize operational processes to improve efficiency and reduce costs. Streamline workflows and eliminate bottlenecks.
- Supply Chain Management: Strengthen your supply chain to ensure a seamless flow of goods and services.
- Establish relationships with reliable suppliers and logistics partners.

6. Customer Experience:

- Maintain Quality: Make sure that, even with the expansion, the calibre of your goods and services is preserved or enhanced.
- Long-term success depends heavily on customer satisfaction.
- Customer Support: To manage the growing volume of inquiries and guarantee a satisfying customer experience, improve customer support services.

7. Promotion and Branding:

- Localized Promotion: Adapt your promotional tactics to the inclinations and requirements of the emerging markets.
- Take into account linguistic and cultural quirks.
- Brand Consistency: Maintain consistency in branding across all markets to reinforce a strong and unified brand image.

8. Legal and Regulatory Compliance:

- Local Regulations: Familiarize yourself with and adhere to local regulations in the new markets. Seek legal advice to ensure compliance with local laws.
- Risk Assessment: Conduct a comprehensive risk assessment to identify legal and regulatory risks associated with the expansion.

8. Communication and Change Management:

- Transparent Communication: Communicate expansion plans transparently with employees, customers, and stakeholders. Provide regular updates on progress and milestones.
- Change Management: Implement effective change management strategies to help employees adapt to new processes, structures, and responsibilities.

9. **Observation and Assessment:**
   - KPIs, or key performance indicators: Create KPIs to gauge the expansion's success. Monitor and assess performance in relation to these metrics on a regular basis.
   - Feedback Systems: Put feedback systems in place to get opinions from stakeholders, consumers, and staff. Utilize this feedback to make the required changes.

10. **Managing Risks:**
- Contingency Planning: Develop contingency plans for potential challenges. Anticipate and plan for various scenarios to ensure resilience during the expansion.
- Insurance: Review and update insurance coverage to mitigate risks associated with the expanded operations.

11. **Adaptive Leadership:**
   Leadership Development: Invest in leadership development programs to equip leaders with the skills needed to guide the organization through expansion.

   Agility: Foster an agile and adaptable organizational culture. Leaders should be responsive to changing circumstances and market dynamics.

13. **Continuous Improvement:**

- Feedback Loops: Establish feedback loops to capture insights from employees, customers, and stakeholders. Use this information to drive continuous improvement.
- Iterative Approach: Adopt an iterative approach to expansion, allowing for flexibility and adjustments based on real-time feedback and data.

14. **Sustainability and Corporate Social Responsibility (CSR):**

- Ethical Practices: Uphold ethical business practices and demonstrate social responsibility. Consider the environmental and social impact of your expanded operations.
- Community Engagement: Engage with local communities in new markets through CSR initiatives that align with your brand values.

Avoiding Common Pitfalls

Expanding a business comes with its share of challenges and potential pitfalls. Being aware of these common pitfalls and proactively addressing them can significantly improve the likelihood of a successful expansion. Here are some common pitfalls to avoid:

1. **Lack of Comprehensive Planning:**

Pitfall: Insufficient planning and a lack of a comprehensive strategy can lead to missteps and unexpected challenges during expansion.

Prevention: Conduct thorough market research, create a detailed business plan, and ensure that all aspects of the expansion are well thought out.

2. **Insufficient Financial Preparation:**

Pitfall: Underestimating the financial requirements of expansion can lead to cash flow problems and financial strain.

Prevention: Develop a detailed budget, conduct financial modelling, and secure adequate funding to support the expansion. Plan for contingencies.

3. **Poor Talent Management:**

Pitfall: Inadequate attention to talent acquisition, training, and development can result in a lack of skilled personnel to support the expanded operations.

Prevention: Implement a robust recruitment and training strategy. Ensure that your team has the necessary skills and capabilities for the expanded roles.

4. Overlooking Cultural Differences:

Pitfall: Ignoring or underestimating cultural differences in new markets can lead to ineffective marketing, communication, and operations.

Prevention: Conduct cultural sensitivity training, tailor marketing strategies to local preferences, and adapt business practices to align with cultural norms.

5. Neglecting Legal and Regulatory Compliance:

Pitfall: Failing to understand and comply with local laws and regulations in new markets can result in legal issues and reputational damage.

Prevention: Seek legal advice, conduct thorough due diligence on regulatory requirements, and ensure that your operations align with local laws.

6. Rapid Scaling Without Testing:

Pitfall: Scaling too quickly without proper testing can lead to operational inefficiencies, customer dissatisfaction, and increased risks.

Prevention: Pilot new initiatives, products, or services before full-scale implementation. Gather feedback and make necessary adjustments.

7. Inadequate Technology Infrastructure:

Pitfall: Neglecting to invest in scalable and robust technology systems can result in operational bottlenecks and difficulties in managing increased workload.

Prevention: Upgrade and invest in technology infrastructure that can handle the expanded operations. Consider cloud-based solutions for scalability.

8. Ignoring Customer Feedback:

Pitfall: Neglecting customer feedback during expansion can lead to misalignment with customer needs and dissatisfaction.

Prevention: Continuously gather and analyse customer feedback. Use this information to make informed decisions and improve products or services.

9. Overreliance on Existing Success:

Pitfall: Assuming that past success guarantees success in new markets or with new products/services can lead to complacency and oversight.

Prevention: Approach each expansion with a fresh perspective. Conduct market research and adapt strategies based on the unique characteristics of the new venture.

10. Poor Communication and Change Management:

Pitfall: Inadequate communication about the expansion with employees and stakeholders can lead to confusion and resistance to change.

Prevention: Communicate transparently about expansion plans, involve employees in the process, and implement effective change management strategies.

11. Lack of Flexibility and Adaptability:

Pitfall: Rigid and inflexible strategies may not account for unforeseen challenges and changes in market conditions.

Prevention: Foster a culture of adaptability and flexibility. Be prepared to adjust strategies based on evolving circumstances.

12. Ignoring Local Competitors:

Pitfall: Underestimating or ignoring local competitors in new markets can lead to ineffective competitive strategies.

Prevention: Conduct a thorough analysis of local competitors. Understand their strengths and weaknesses to formulate effective market entry strategies.

13. Overlooking Sustainability and CSR:

Pitfall: Neglecting environmental and social responsibility considerations can result in negative public perception and regulatory issues.

Prevention: Integrate sustainable practices and corporate social responsibility into your expansion plans. Demonstrate a commitment to ethical business practices.

14. **Failure to Learn from Mistakes:**

- **Pitfall**: Failing to learn from mistakes made during expansion can lead to repeated errors and hinder future success.
- **Prevention**: Establish a culture of continuous improvement. Conduct post-expansion evaluations, gather feedback, and use lessons learned to refine future strategies.

15. **Inadequate Risk Management:**

Pitfall: Ignoring or downplaying potential risks associated with expansion can lead to significant setbacks.

Prevention: Conduct thorough

Adaptability and Innovation

Adaptability and innovation are key drivers of success, especially in dynamic and ever-changing business environments. These traits enable businesses to navigate challenges, stay competitive, and seize new opportunities. Here's a closer look at adaptability and innovation:

Adaptability:

- **Definition:** Adaptability is the ability of individuals or organizations to adjust to new conditions, changes, or challenges. It involves being flexible, open-minded, and responsive to shifts in the environment.
- **Importance**: In a rapidly changing business landscape, adaptability is crucial for survival. It allows organizations to respond to market trends, customer preferences, and external factors effectively.
- **Techniques for Fostering Flexibility**: Culture of Constant Learning: Foster an environment where learning never stops. Give staff members opportunities for training and development so they can learn new skills and information.
- **Promote Open Communication**: Encourage channels of open communication. Encourage staff members to voice their thoughts, opinions, and worries in order to foster a culture that values flexibility.

• **Agile Methodologies**: Project management should use agile methodologies. Agile development facilitates adaptation to changes quickly, flexibility, and iterative development.

- **Planning scenarios** Prepare scenarios in advance to foresee obstacles and create plans for a range of potential outcomes.

Innovation

- **Definition:** Innovation is the process of developing and putting into practice fresh concepts, procedures, goods, or services that benefit people, companies, or society as a whole.
- **Importance:** Growth and competitiveness are fuelled by innovation. Innovative companies stay ahead of the curve, adapt to changing consumer needs, and frequently upend entire industries.
- Methods for Promoting Innovation: Foster an Innovation Culture: Establish a setting that rewards innovation and daring. Reward and acknowledge creative thinking and hard work.
- **Cross-functional Collaboration**: Promote cooperation between various teams and departments. Creative solutions are frequently the result of diverse perspectives.
- Investing in research and development entails allocating resources to these endeavors. Investigating novel technologies, procedures, or business prospects may fall under this category.
- Customer-Centric Innovation: Pay attention to what customers have to say and include them in the process of innovation. Recognize their preferences and needs to develop solutions that work for them.

The Relationship between Innovation and Adaptability:

1. Feedback Loop:

Adaptability and innovation create a feedback loop. Being adaptable allows an organization to respond to changes and challenges identified through innovation, and innovation, in turn, drives continuous adaptation.

2. Resilience:

The combination of adaptability and innovation enhances organizational resilience. Instead of simply reacting to changes, businesses can proactively shape their future by innovating in response to evolving circumstances.

3. Competitive Edge:

Organizations that are both adaptable and innovative gain a competitive edge. They are better positioned to anticipate market trends, meet customer demands, and outperform competitors.

4. Employee Engagement:

Employees in adaptable and innovative environments are often more engaged. They feel a sense of purpose and contribute to a culture of continuous improvement.

5. Risk Mitigation:

Adaptability helps businesses mitigate risks associated with changes, while innovation enables them to identify and capitalize on new opportunities, reducing reliance on existing strategies.

Chapter 19

Navigating Change

Navigating change is a critical skill for individuals and organizations alike, particularly in today's dynamic and evolving environments. Whether dealing with technological advancements, market shifts, or internal transformations, effective navigation of change requires strategic planning, clear communication, and a focus on adaptability.

A combination of people-centeredness, good communication, and strategic planning are needed to navigate change successfully. Through employee involvement, addressing resistance, and cultivating an adaptable culture, organizations can effectively manage change and position themselves for long-term success in dynamic environments.

Here's a guide on navigating change:

1. **Understand the Need for Change**:
   - Assessment: Conduct a thorough assessment to understand the reasons behind the need for change. This could involve analyzing market trends, identifying internal inefficiencies, or responding to external factors.
   - Clearly Stated Goals: • Establish the change's clearly stated goals. What do you hope to accomplish? Setting clear objectives aids in directing the entire change process.
2. **Form a Group for Change Management:**
   - Cross-Functional Team: To spearhead the change initiatives, form a cross-functional team. People with varying perspectives and skill sets from various departments should be on this team.
   - Leadership Support: Obtain resolute backing from the leaders within the organization. Their dedication to the change is essential to fostering employee confidence.
3. **Openness and Communication:**

- Open Communication: Talk freely about the need for change, its justifications, and its anticipated advantages. Transparency helps control expectations and fosters trust.
- Two-Way Communication: Promote two-way dialogue. Permit staff members to voice their worries, pose inquiries, and offer feedback.

4. **Develop a Comprehensive Change Plan**:

- Timeline and Milestones: Create a detailed plan that includes a timeline and specific milestones. This helps in tracking progress and ensures that the change process is well-managed.
- Resource Allocation: Allocate the necessary resources, including financial, technological, and human resources, to support the change initiatives.

5. **Provide Training and Support:**

- Skill Development: Offer training programs to help employees develop the skills needed for the changes. This could involve technical training, soft skills development, or leadership training.

Mental Health Support: Acknowledge that change can be stressful. Provide resources for mental health support, such as counselling services or workshops.

6. **Celebrate Small Wins:**

- Recognition: Celebrate and recognize small wins along the way. Acknowledging achievements boosts morale and helps maintain momentum during the change process.
- Positive Reinforcement: Reinforce the positive aspects of the change. Highlight how it contributes to the organization's goals and benefits employees.

7. **Monitor and Adjust:**

- Key Performance Indicators (KPIs):
- Establish key performance indicators to measure the success of the change. Regularly monitor these indicators and adjust strategies as needed.
- Feedback Loops: Implement feedback mechanisms to gather insights from employees and stakeholders. Use this feedback to make informed adjustments to the change plan.

8. **Address Resistance:**

- Identify Resistance: Recognize and understand that resistance to change is natural. Identify the sources of resistance and address them proactively.
- Communication of Benefits: Clearly communicate the benefits of the change. Help employees understand how the change aligns with organizational goals and their individual success.

8. **Foster a Culture of Adaptability:**

- Continuous Learning: Encourage a culture of continuous learning. Emphasize the importance of staying adaptable and responsive to changes in the business environment.
- Innovation: Tie the change efforts to a culture of innovation. Demonstrate how the organization's willingness to change contributes to its ability to innovate.

10. **Evaluate and Reflect:**

- Post-Change Evaluation: After the change has been implemented, conduct a thorough evaluation. Assess what worked well, what could be improved, and what lessons can be applied to future changes.
- Learning Organization: Foster a learning organization mindset, where the organization continually learns from its experiences and adapts accordingly.

Embracing Innovation

Embracing innovation is essential for organizations looking to stay competitive, adapt to evolving markets, and drive sustainable growth. It takes a sustained commitment to stay ahead of the curve to embrace innovation rather than a one-time effort. Organizations can establish themselves as leaders in their fields and bring about significant change by promoting a culture that values creativity, giving access to the resources they need, and promoting cooperation.

Here are key strategies for embracing innovation:

1. **Create a Culture of Innovation:**

- Leadership Support: Leaders should actively support and promote a culture of innovation. Their commitment sets the tone for the entire organization.
- Promote Risk-Taking: Cultivate an atmosphere that rewards measured risks-taking. Workers ought to be confident enough to put forth fresh ideas without worrying about failing.
- Reward and Recognition: Acknowledge and honour creative endeavors. This could take the form of rewards, recognition during team gatherings, or even prizes for inventiveness.

2. **Create Interdepartmental Cooperation**

- Diverse Teams: Assemble cross-functional groups comprising individuals from various departments and backgrounds. Creative solutions are frequently the result of diverse perspectives.
- Encourage open communication between teams by promoting open communication. Dismantling organizational silos promotes cooperation and lets ideas circulate throughout the whole company.

3. **Provide Resources for Innovation:**

- Investment in Research and Development: Allocate resources, both financial and human, to research and development efforts. This could involve exploring new technologies, processes, or market opportunities.
- Innovation Labs or Spaces: Create dedicated spaces or labs where employees can collaborate and work on innovative projects.

4. **Encourage Continuous Learning:**

- Training Programs: Offer training programs to enhance employees' skills and knowledge. This could include workshops on new technologies, methodologies, or creative problem-solving.

5. **Learning Opportunities**:

- Provide access to learning opportunities, such as conferences, webinars, and courses, to stay updated on industry trends and best practices.

6. **Pay Attention to Customer Feedback**:

- Customer-Centric Innovation: Engage customers in the process of innovation by actively listening to their opinions. For solutions to be created that add value, it is essential to comprehend their needs and pain points.

- User Experience (UX) Testing: To learn more about how customers use goods or services, conduct UX testing. Make improvements and iterations using this knowledge.

7. **Embrace Technology**:

  - Digital Transformation: • Adopt new technologies that can improve workflows, boost productivity, and produce cutting-edge goods and services.

  - Data Analytics: Make use of data analytics to learn about market trends, consumer behaviour, and areas that require development. Making decisions based on data is a crucial component of innovation.

8. **Establish Innovation Challenges**:

  - Idea Generation Challenges: Arrange innovation challenges or hackathons where staff members can provide concepts and collaborate to address particular issues.

  - Innovation Competitions: Hold internal competitions for innovative ideas and provide rewards for the most impactful and promising submissions.

9. **Joint Ventures and Partnerships:**

   External Collaboration: To bring new ideas and perspectives into the company, work with startups, outside partners, or industry experts. Investigate open innovation models that draw inspiration from a wider ecosystem that encompasses suppliers, customers, and outside experts.

10. Put Agile Techniques into Practice:

- Agile Frameworks: • Implement agile project management techniques. Agile development facilitates adaptation to changes quickly, flexibility, and iterative development.
- Scrum Teams: Assemble groups of people into compact, multidisciplinary scrum teams that are able to cooperate and adjust to shifting priorities.

11. Calculate and Assess:

- KPIs, or key performance indicators: Create key performance indicators to gauge how well innovation initiatives are working. Assess performance against these metrics on a regular basis.
- Feedback Mechanisms: Use feedback mechanisms to get opinions and insights from stakeholders, consumers, and staff. Make wise adjustments using this information.

Chapter 20

Staying Competitive

Staying competitive in today's dynamic business environment requires a strategic and adaptive approach. Here are key strategies to help organizations stay competitive:

1. **Continuous Market Analysis:**

- Stay Informed: Regularly analyse market trends, industry developments, and competitor activities. Stay informed about changes in customer preferences and emerging technologies.

- Competitor Analysis: Conduct thorough competitor analysis to understand their strengths, weaknesses, opportunities, and threats. Identify areas where your organization can differentiate itself.

2. **Customer-Centric Approach**:

- Customer Feedback: Actively seek and listen to customer feedback. Use customer insights to improve products, services, and overall customer experience.

- Personalization: Implement personalized marketing strategies and offerings based on customer preferences. Tailor your products or services to meet specific needs.

3. **Innovation and Technology Adoption:**

- Invest in Research and Development: Allocate resources to research and development efforts. Explore new technologies and innovative solutions to enhance products or services.

- Digital Transformation: Incorporate technology into all facets of the company's operations, including customer interactions, to fully embrace digital transformation.

4. **Adaptable and nimble Activities:**

- Agile Methodologies: Project managers can improve their flexibility and responsiveness to market changes by implementing agile methodologies.

Ensure that the supply chain is adaptable and efficient to promptly respond to shifts in market conditions, disruptions, and demand.

5. **Acquisition of Talent:**

- Acquire knowledge continuously by making investments in staff members' continuing education and training. Give them the tools they need to change with the times and adjust to new technologies and industry standards.
- Recruit and retain outstanding personnel. Being competitive requires having a workforce that is both skilled and motivated.

6. **Strategic Partnerships**:

  - Work with Industry Leaders: Establish strategic alliances with other companies, such as startups, research institutions, or industry leaders. Innovative solutions and competitive advantages can arise from collaborative efforts.
  - Supplier Relationships: Cultivate a solid rapport with suppliers. Work together closely to guarantee a reliable and effective supply chain.

7. **Brand Positioning and Marketing**:

  - Distinguishing yourself from the competition: • Clearly state and convey your special selling point. Establish a distinct brand identity from rivals to establish a dominant market position.
  - Digital marketing: • Use efficient digital marketing techniques to interact with clients through a variety of online platforms and reach a larger audience.

8. **Finance Management:**

  - Cost Efficiency: Constantly assess and maximize operating expenses. Seek ways to increase productivity without sacrificing quality.
  - Financial Planning: To guarantee stability and adaptability in handling economic uncertainties, create strong financial planning techniques.

9. **Regulatory Compliance**:

  - Keep abreast of industry regulations and compliance needs. Be compliant. Make sure that your operations follow the law in order to stay out of trouble and protect your reputation.

10. **Making Decisions Based on Data:**
- Data Analytics: Use data analytics to help you make wise choices. To inform strategic initiatives, evaluate performance metrics, market trends, and customer data.
- Predictive Analytics: To predict consumer behaviour and market trends, investigate predictive analytics. Position your company proactively using insights derived from data.

11. **Risk Management:**
- Risk Assessment: Conduct regular risk assessments to identify potential challenges and threats. Develop mitigation strategies to navigate uncertainties.
- Crisis Management: Establish crisis management plans to respond effectively to unexpected challenges, ensuring minimal disruption to operations.

12. **Corporate Social Responsibility (CSR):**
- Social Impact: Integrate CSR initiatives that align with your organization's values. A positive social impact can enhance brand reputation and customer loyalty.
- Environmental Sustainability: Consider environmentally sustainable practices. Green initiatives can appeal to environmentally conscious consumers.

13. **E-commerce and Online Presence:**
- E-commerce Integration: If applicable, enhance your e-commerce capabilities. Facilitate online transactions, providing customers with convenient and accessible purchasing options.
- Digital Platforms: Maintain a strong online presence through various digital platforms. Engage with customers through social media, websites, and other online channels.

14. **Adaptability and Future Readiness:**
- Strategic Planning: Develop long-term strategic plans that consider future trends and potential disruptions. Position your organization to adapt to evolving industry landscapes.
- Technological Readiness: Stay technologically ready by regularly updating systems, adopting emerging technologies, and anticipating the impact of technological advancements on your industry.

To remain competitive, one must adopt a comprehensive and progressive strategy. Organizations can position themselves for long-term success in a business environment that is changing quickly by consistently adjusting to market dynamics, giving customers' needs top priority, encouraging innovation, and upholding financial stability.

Chapter 21

Social Responsibility and Ethics

In order to conduct business in a way that goes beyond simple profitability, social responsibility and ethics are essential components.

Enterprises that adopt social responsibility and ethical standards make valuable contributions to the community, cultivate confidence among interested parties, and improve their enduring viability.

The following is a manual on business ethics and social responsibility:

Civic Duty:

1. Interpretation:

• A company's commitment to upholding moral principles and promoting societal welfare is referred to as social responsibility. The process entails taking into account how business decisions will affect different stakeholders, such as customers, employees, communities, and the environment.

2. Important Social Responsibility Aspects:

Corporate philanthropy entails the following: • Take part in social initiatives, support community projects, and donate to charitable causes.

• Environmental Sustainability: Reduce the ecological impact of business operations by implementing environmentally sustainable practices. This entails using green technologies, minimizing waste, and conserving resources.

• Community Engagement: Take an active part in your neighbourhood communities. This could entail funding nearby companies, endorsing events, and taking part in initiatives for community improvement.

•   Ethical Employment Practices:

•   Ensure fair and ethical employment practices, including diversity and inclusion initiatives, fair wages, and a safe working environment.

Ethics in Business:

1. Definition: Ethics in business involves adhering to a set of moral principles and values in decision-making and operations. Ethical behaviour goes beyond legal requirements and aims to uphold integrity, honesty, and fairness.

2. Key Principles of Business Ethics:

•   Integrity: Uphold integrity in all business dealings. Be honest, transparent, and truthful in communication and actions.

•   Fairness: Treat all stakeholders fairly and without discrimination. Ensure that decisions are unbiased and just.

•   Accountability: Take responsibility for the consequences of business decisions. Acknowledge mistakes, learn from them, and take corrective actions.

•   Respect for Individuals: Show respect for the dignity and rights of individuals, both within the organization and in external relationships.

3. Practical Applications:

•   Ethical Decision-Making: Establish a framework for ethical decision-making within the organization. Encourage employees to consider ethical implications in their professional conduct.

•   Code of Conduct: Create and distribute a thorough code of conduct outlining the moral expectations for each and every employee.

4. Protection for Whistleblowers: Put in place safeguards to shield those who expose unethical activity. Establish a culture that values reporting unethical behaviour.

Advantages of Ethics and Social Responsibility:

1. **Enhanced Reputation**: Businesses that place a high value on ethics and social responsibility cultivate a favourable reputation that can inspire greater confidence in stakeholders, workers, and clients.

2. **Loyalty of Customers**: Consumers are becoming more attracted to ethical companies. Businesses can attract socially conscious customers and increase customer loyalty by exhibiting social responsibility.

3. **Employee Satisfaction**: When an organization prioritizes social responsibility and ethical practices, its workforce is more likely to be engaged and satisfied.

4.**Risk Mitigation**: Legal and reputational risks can be reduced by upholding moral principles and participating in socially conscious activities.

5. **Competitive Advantage**: By setting a company apart in the market and drawing clients who share its values, social responsibility can give a company a competitive edge.

6. **Long-Term Sustainability**: Businesses that prioritize ethics and social responsibility are better positioned to achieve long-term sustainability. In the face of difficulties and modifications to the business environment, they exhibit greater resilience.

Obstacles and Things to Think About:

1. **Juggling the Interests of Stakeholders**:

•Businesses must weigh the interests of different stakeholders, taking into account how decisions will affect shareholders, customers, staff, and the community at large.

2. **Global Considerations**: Companies that conduct business internationally must negotiate a variety of cultural and ethical environments. Respecting and comprehending cultural differences is essential for making moral decisions.

3. **Measuring Impact**: It can be difficult to gauge the success of social responsibility programs. The positive contributions can be quantified with the establishment of precise metrics and evaluation frameworks.

It is not only morally required but also a calculated strategic decision for businesses to incorporate social responsibility and ethics into their operations. Organizations can cultivate a positive corporate culture, gain the trust of stakeholders, and achieve long-term sustainable success by coordinating their business operations with moral standards and making constructive contributions to the community.

Corporate Social Responsibility

Corporate Social Responsibility (CSR) is a business approach that goes beyond profit-making and encompasses the impact of an organization's activities on society and the environment. CSR involves integrating ethical, social, and environmental considerations into business operations and decision-making.

Here's an overview of Corporate Social Responsibility:

Key Components of Corporate Social Responsibility:

1. Environmental Sustainability:

- Initiatives: Implement eco-friendly practices, reduce carbon footprint, and support environmental conservation projects.

- Compliance: Adhere to environmental regulations and seek ways to minimize negative environmental impacts.

2. Social Well-being:

- Community Engagement: Actively participate in community development projects, support local initiatives, and contribute to the well-being of the communities in which the organization operates.

- Philanthropy: Contribute to charitable causes, donate to nonprofits, and engage in philanthropic activities.

3. Ethical Business Practices:

- Code of Conduct: Develop and adhere to a comprehensive code of conduct that outlines ethical standards for employees and the organization.

- Anti-corruption Measures: Implement measures to prevent corruption, bribery, and unethical business practices.

4. **Employee Well-being**:

•	Fair Employment Practices: Ensure fair wages, provide safe working conditions, and promote diversity and inclusion within the workforce.

•	Employee Development: Invest in employee training, professional development, and overall well-being.

5. **Stakeholder Engagement**:

•	Transparency: Communicate openly with stakeholders about business practices, goals, and performance.

•	Listening Mechanisms: Establish mechanisms for listening to and addressing the concerns of various stakeholders, including customers, employees, and communities.

6. **Product Responsibility**:

•	Product Safety: Ensure the safety and quality of products. Adhere to regulations and industry standards.

•	Innovation for Social Good: Develop products or services that contribute positively to society or address social challenges.

Benefits of Corporate Social Responsibility:

1.	**Enhanced Reputation**:

•	Organizations engaged in CSR activities often enjoy a positive reputation, leading to increased trust and goodwill among customers and stakeholders.

2.	**Customer Loyalty**:

•	Socially responsible practices can build customer loyalty, as consumers are increasingly inclined to support businesses that align with their values.

3.	**Employee Engagement**:

•	CSR initiatives contribute to a positive workplace culture, leading to higher employee satisfaction, engagement, and retention.

4.	**Risk Management**:

*   Proactive CSR measures can mitigate risks associated with legal and regulatory compliance, as well as reputational risks.

5.   **Competitive Advantage**:

*   Demonstrating a commitment to social responsibility can differentiate a business in the marketplace and provide a competitive edge.

6.   **Long-Term Sustainability**:

*   CSR contributes to the long-term sustainability of an organization by fostering resilience and adaptability to changing societal and environmental dynamics.

Challenges and Criticisms of CSR

1.   Greenwashing:

*   Some organizations may engage in "greenwashing," where they exaggerate or misrepresent their commitment to environmental sustainability for marketing purposes.

2.   Resource Allocation:

*   Balancing CSR initiatives with financial and operational considerations can be challenging. Organizations must carefully allocate resources to ensure effectiveness.

3.   Global Complexity:

*   Multinational corporations face the challenge of navigating diverse cultural, legal, and social landscapes when implementing CSR initiatives across different countries.

4.   Measuring Impact:

*   Quantifying the social and environmental impact of CSR initiatives can be complex, and measuring success may involve subjective criteria.

<u>**Reporting and Communication**</u>:

- **CSR Reporting**: Many organizations publish annual CSR reports to transparently communicate their initiatives, progress, and impact.

- **Communication Channels**: Utilize various communication channels, including websites, social media, and public relations, to share CSR activities with stakeholders.

A dynamic and ever-evolving concept, corporate social responsibility represents a dedication to moral business conduct and constructive contributions to society. Adopting CSR is a strategic decision that can result in sustainable business practices and long-term success in addition to being morally required. Businesses that incorporate corporate social responsibility (CSR) into their basic principles help create a more socially and ecologically conscious global business environment.

Ethical Decision-Making

Ethical decision-making involves a process of evaluating and choosing among alternatives in a manner consistent with ethical principles. It requires considering the potential impact of decisions on various stakeholders and aligning choices with moral values and standards.

Here is a guide to ethical decision-making:

1. Clarify the Decision:

- Define the Problem:

- Clearly articulate the ethical dilemma or issue that requires a decision. Identify the key factors and individuals involved.

- Gather Information:

- Collect relevant information about the situation. Consider the facts, potential consequences, and the perspectives of different stakeholders.

2. Identify Stakeholders:

- List Stakeholders:

- Identify and list all individuals or groups who may be affected by the decision. This could include employees, customers, shareholders, and the broader community.

- Consider Interests:

- Understand the interests, concerns, and values of each stakeholder. Recognize the potential impact of the decision on their well-being.

3. Evaluate Options:

- Generate Alternatives:

- Brainstorm potential solutions or courses of action. Consider a range of options that could address the ethical dilemma.

- Apply Ethical Principles:

- Evaluate each alternative against ethical principles such as honesty, integrity, fairness, and respect for individuals. Consider how each option aligns with your organization's values.

4. Consider Consequences:

- Short-Term vs. Long-Term Impact:

- Assess the short-term and long-term consequences of each option. Consider potential positive and negative outcomes for all stakeholders.

- Unintended Consequences:

- Anticipate unintended consequences of each decision. Assess how the decision might impact individuals or groups not initially identified.

5. Seek Guidance:

- Consult Colleagues or Experts:

- Seek input from colleagues, mentors, or subject matter experts. Discussing the ethical dilemma with others can provide diverse perspectives and insights.

- Review Organizational Policies:

- Check if there are existing organizational policies or codes of conduct that provide guidance on similar ethical issues.

6. Make the Decision:

- Prioritize Ethical Considerations:

- Prioritize ethical considerations in the decision-making process. Choose the alternative that best aligns with ethical principles and values.

- Take Responsibility:

- Accept responsibility for the decision. Acknowledge that ethical decision-making involves personal accountability for the chosen course of action.

7. Communicate the Decision:

- Transparent Communication:

- Communicate the decision transparently to all relevant stakeholders. Provide clear and honest explanations for the chosen course of action.

- Address Concerns:

- Address concerns or questions from stakeholders. Demonstrate a commitment to openness and accountability.

8. Implement the Decision:

- Execute the Plan:

- Implement the chosen course of action in a timely and effective manner. Ensure that all necessary steps are taken to execute the decision.

- Monitor Progress:

- Monitor the implementation process to ensure that it aligns with the ethical considerations and achieves the desired outcomes.

9. Reflect and Learn:

- Post-Decision Reflection:

- Reflect on the decision-making process. Consider what worked well and what could be improved for future ethical dilemmas.

- Continuous Improvement:

- Use the experience to enhance the organization's approach to ethical decision-making. Identify opportunities for continuous improvement in ethical practices.

10. Review and Adjust:

- Feedback Mechanisms:

- Establish feedback mechanisms to gather input from stakeholders about the decision and its impact. Use this feedback to make adjustments if necessary.

- Adapt to Changing Circumstances:

- Recognize that ethical decision-making is an ongoing process. Adapt and refine approaches based on changing circumstances and new information.

A dynamic and iterative process, ethical decision-making entails giving serious thought to the ideals and tenets that steer an organization. Individuals and organizations can navigate complex dilemmas in a way that is consistent with their moral compass and fosters a culture of integrity and responsibility by adhering to a structured approach and giving ethical considerations priority.

Chapter 22

Building a Purpose-Driven Business

Building a purpose-driven business involves aligning the organization's mission and values with a broader social or environmental purpose. It goes beyond profit-making and emphasizes making a positive impact on society.

 Here's a guide to building a purpose-driven business:

1. Define Your Purpose:

•	Mission Statement:

•	Clearly articulate your organization's mission and purpose. Define the positive impact you aim to make in the world.

•	Values and Principles:

•	Identify core values and principles that guide decision-making and actions. Ensure that these values align with your purpose.

2. Embed Purpose in Culture:

•	Leadership Commitment:

•	Demonstrate strong leadership commitment to the organization's purpose. Leaders should embody the values and principles in their actions.

•	Employee Engagement:

•	Foster a culture where employees feel connected to the purpose. Encourage their involvement in initiatives that contribute to the organization's broader mission.

3. Integrate Purpose into Strategy:

•	Strategic Alignment:

•	Align your business strategy with your purpose. Consider how each aspect of your operations contributes to achieving your broader mission.

- Long-Term Vision:

- Develop a long-term vision that reflects your commitment to making a positive impact. Outline how your purpose will guide the growth and development of the business.

4. **Stakeholder Engagement**:

- Customer Relationships:

- Build relationships with customers based on shared values. Communicate your purpose and involve customers in supporting your mission.

- Community Involvement:

- Engage with local communities and other stakeholders. Demonstrate a commitment to social and environmental responsibility.

5. **Ethical and Sustainable Practices:**

- Sustainability Initiatives:

- Implement sustainable business practices. Consider the environmental impact of your operations and seek ways to reduce your carbon footprint.

- Ethical Sourcing:

- Prioritize ethical sourcing of materials and ensure fair labour practices throughout your supply chain.

6. **Measure and Report Impact**:

- Key Performance Indicators (KPIs):

- Establish KPIs to measure the impact of your purpose-driven initiatives. This could include social, environmental, and community-related metrics.

- Transparency:

- Communicate openly about your organization's impact. Publish reports and updates on how you are fulfilling your purpose.

7. **Social Innovation**:

- Innovative Solutions:

• Encourage an innovative culture to create goods and services that tackle environmental or social issues.

Cooperation: To increase your influence, work with partners, non-governmental organizations, or other organizations. Combine resources and knowledge to promote constructive change.

8. **Work-Life Balance and Employee Well-Being**: Give these two factors top priority. Make sure that your team's physical and mental well-being are supported at work.

9. **Training and Development**: Invest in your staff members' professional growth. Offer chances for development and skill-building that are in line with your mission.

10. **Using a customer-centric approach**, you should: educate customers about your mission and how their support helps bring about positive change. Encourage a feeling of collective accountability.

11. **Receptive to Feedback**: Pay attention to what customers have to say and address their issues. Utilize feedback from customers to improve

<u>Adaptability and Ongoing Improvement:</u>

- Adjust to Changing Requirements: Remain flexible and sensitive to changing environmental and social requirements. Be prepared to modify your plans in light of fresh knowledge and evolving situations.
- Culture of Continuous Learning: Establish a culture that values ongoing education. Motivate the company to look for methods to get better and learn from its mistakes.
- Developing a purpose-driven company necessitates a comprehensive strategy that incorporates purpose into every facet of the enterprise. Businesses may achieve long-term success and sustainability while making a significant contribution to society by integrating stakeholders, measuring impact, and matching values with actions.

Chapter 23

Exit Strategies Techniques

Business owners create exit strategies as a means of selling their company or pulling out of a specific project. For investors and entrepreneurs, having a well-thought-out exit strategy is crucial because it offers a path for optimizing profits and leaving the company. Here are a few typical exit tactics:

1. **The first public offering, or IPO:**

- **Definition**: • Listing a private company's shares on a stock exchange allows it to become public. As a result, the ownership of the business can be traded openly.
- **When to Think About It**: Usually sought after by bigger, more established businesses looking to raise a sizable sum of money and with a strong track record of financial stability.

- **Pros**: Access to a broader pool of capital.

- Increased liquidity for existing shareholders.

- Enhanced visibility and credibility.

- **Cons:** Significant regulatory requirements.

- High costs associated with the IPO process.

- Continuous public scrutiny and reporting obligations.

2. **Merger or Acquisition:**

- Definition: Selling the business to another company (acquisition) or merging with another company. This can provide liquidity to the existing owners.

- **When to Consider**: When there's interest from another company looking to acquire or merge.

- When the business has achieved a level of success that makes it an attractive target.

- **Pros**: Immediate liquidity for owners.

- Access to the resources of a larger company.

- Potential for synergies and growth opportunities.

- **Cons:** Loss of control for the original owners.

- Integration challenges.

- Negotiation complexities.

3. **Management Buyout (MBO) or Employee Stock Ownership Plan (ESOP)**:

- MBO Definition: The existing management team acquires the business from the current owners.

- ESOP Definition: The company creates a trust to hold shares on behalf of employees, making them partial owners.

- **When to Consider**: MBO: When the current management team is interested in taking over.

- ESOP: As a succession planning strategy or to enhance employee engagement.

- **Pros:** Smooth transition with existing management.

- May provide favourable tax treatment.

- Employees become stakeholders in the company.

- **Cons:** Financing challenges for MBO.

- Potential for conflicts within the management team.

- ESOP requires ongoing administration and communication.

4. **Liquidation**:

- Definition: Closing down the business and selling off its assets. This is often considered when the business is not financially viable.

- **When to Consider**: When the business is no longer profitable or sustainable.

- When there are no viable buyers or investors.

*   **Pros:** Provides a way to wind down the business and distribute remaining assets.

*   Allows owners to minimize losses in a failing venture.

*   **Cons:** Limited returns compared to other exit strategies.

*   May involve legal and financial complexities.

*   Loss of invested time and effort.

5. **Strategic Alliances or Joint Ventures**:

*   Definition: Collaborating with another company in a strategic alliance or joint venture, which can lead to shared ownership or an eventual merger.

*   **When to Consider**: When there are opportunities for collaboration that can drive mutual growth.

*   As a precursor to a potential merger or acquisition.

*   **Pros**: Access to complementary resources and expertise.

*   Shared risks and rewards.

*   Can be a strategic stepping stone toward a larger transaction.

*   **Cons:** Requires effective negotiation and alignment of interests.

*   Potential for conflicts in decision-making.

*   Not a standalone exit strategy but a precursor to others.

6. **Franchising:**

*   Definition: Expanding the business by granting licenses to third parties (franchisees) to operate outlets under the brand.

*   **When to Consider**: When the business model is easily replicable.

*   When there is demand for the brand in other locations.

*   **Pros:** Rapid expansion without significant capital investment.

*   Franchisees contribute to the brand's success.

- Potential for ongoing royalty income.

- **Cons:** Requires a well-established and replicable business model.

- Ongoing support and monitoring of franchisees are essential.

- Loss of control over individual franchise operations.

Considerations for Choosing an Exit Strategy:

Collaborating with financial advisors, legal experts, and other professionals can prove advantageous when navigating the intricacies of the selected exit strategy.

It is important to carefully consider the objectives and particular circumstances of the business and its owners when choosing the best exit strategy.

1. Timing: The success and value of the selected strategy can be greatly impacted by choosing the appropriate moment to exit.

2. Financial Objectives: Ensure that the exit strategy selected is in line with the owners' and stakeholders' financial objectives.

3. Market Conditions: When deciding on an exit strategy, take the current state of the market and industry trends into account.

4. Business Performance: The company's success and financial standing will affect how appealing it is to prospective investors or buyers.

5. Owner Preferences: Take into account the preferences of the company's owners, such as their wish for continued involvement, their financial targets, and their personal aspirations.

6. Legal and Tax Implications: To comprehend the legal and tax ramifications of the selected exit strategy, speak with financial and legal experts.

7. Legacy and Impact: Take into account the financial success and societal contributions that business owners hope to leave behind, as well as the legacy they want to leave.

Chapter 24

Selling Your Business

Selling a business is a difficult process that needs to be carefully planned, organized, and carried out. A successful business sale requires a number of steps, regardless of your motivations—retirement, taking advantage of new opportunities, or something else entirely. This is a how-to guide for selling your company:

1. Getting ready:

• Financial Documentation: Make sure all of your financial records are current, accurate, and arranged neatly. Financial statements, tax returns, and other pertinent paperwork fall under this category.

• Valuation: Establish the worth of your company. Take into account elements like earnings, profitability, market circumstances, and industry benchmarks.

• Tighten Up Your Finances: Resolve any unresolved legal or contractual issues, straighten up your balance sheet, and attend to any outstanding financial issues.

• Organizational Structure: Make sure your documentation and organizational structure are clear. This covers agreements, contracts, and organizational diagrams.

2. **Identify Your Selling Strategy**:

•	Asset Sale vs. Share Sale: Decide whether you'll sell the assets of the business or the shares of the company. This decision can have tax implications and affect the terms of the sale.

•	Timing: Determine the right time to sell based on market conditions, the financial health of your business, and personal considerations.

3. **Professional Advisors**:

•	Hire Professionals: Engage professionals such as business brokers, attorneys, and accountants with experience in business sales to guide you through the process.

- Confidentiality Agreements: Establish confidentiality agreements to safeguard private information with important personnel and possible purchasers.

4. **Marketing Your Company**:

   - Write a Sales Memorandum: Craft an elaborate sales memorandum that accentuates the salient attributes and fiscal outcomes of your enterprise. Usually, this document is distributed to prospective purchasers.
   - Online Listings: Include a listing for your company on business-for-sale websites, business brokers, and pertinent online platforms.
   - Targeted Marketing: Determine and focus on possible customers, investors, and others with an interest in your sector.

5. **Negotiation**:

   - Be ready to discuss and have reasonable expectations about the terms and conditions as well as the sale price.
   - Letter of Intent (LOI): If a buyer expresses interest, you might get a Letter of Intent detailing the main parameters of the agreement. Let's go over and work out the terms first.

6. **Due Diligence:**

   - Information Provision: Provide the required information, supporting documentation, and access to important personnel in order to assist the buyer's due diligence process.
   - Legal and Financial Review: You should anticipate a comprehensive examination of your operational, financial, and legal aspects.
   - Respond to any issues that surface during the investigation.

7. **Concluding the Transaction**:

   - Acquisition Contract: Create a thorough purchase agreement that details all of the terms and conditions of the sale by working with legal experts.
   - Closing: Arrange for a closing date when ownership is formally transferred and all required paperwork is signed.

8. **The Transition After Sale**:

- Interact with Workers: Be open and honest with your staff about the sale, and give them hope for the future with the new owner.
- Assistance with Transition: Ensure that the new owner receives all the required assistance with transition, such as training, client introductions, and support during the handover phase.

9. **Legal and Tax Points to Remember**:

- Legal Compliance: Verify that the sale conforms with all applicable laws and regulations, including any necessary regulatory approvals.
- Tax Implications: To comprehend the tax ramifications of the sale and investigate ways to reduce tax liabilities, speak with tax professionals.

10. **Take A Lesson from the Event**:

- Think and Learn: Consider the selling procedure. Think back on the successful aspects, identify areas for improvement, and draw lessons for upcoming transactions.

Chapter 25

Success Advice

Selling a business is a significant undertaking, and careful planning and execution are crucial for a successful and profitable transaction. Each business sale is unique, so adapt these steps to fit the specific circumstances of your business and market conditions.

1. **Start Early**: Begin the preparation process well in advance to address any issues and present your business in the best possible light.
2. **Maintain Confidentiality**: Keep the sale confidential until a formal agreement is in place to protect the interests of your business and employees.
3. Be Transparent: Be transparent and honest with potential buyers. Misrepresentation can lead to legal issues and damage your reputation.
4. **Build a Strong Management Team:** Having a competent and stable management team in place can make the business more attractive to potential buyers.
5. **Consider Earn-Outs**: In certain situations, consider structuring the deal with an earn-out arrangement, where a portion of the sale price is contingent on future performance.
6. **Seek Professional Advice**: Engage experienced professionals to guide you through the process, including legal advisors, accountants, and business brokers.

Succession Planning

In order to secure a company's long-term viability and success, succession planning is essential for identifying and training candidates for important positions inside the company. It entails minimizing disruptions to business operations, ensuring a seamless leadership transition, and strategically selecting and grooming leaders in order to prepare for the future. The following is a succession planning guide:

1. **Get Going Early**:

• Long-Term View: Viewing succession planning as a long-term strategy will maximize its effectiveness. Initiate the procedure at an early stage to facilitate the recognition and cultivation of prospective leaders.

2. **Determine Crucial Roles**:

• Crucial Roles: Determine which leadership positions and responsibilities are essential to the company's success and survival.

4. **Evaluate Current Talent**:

- Skills and Competencies: To identify individuals with leadership potential, evaluate the skills, competencies, and potential of current staff members.
- Conduct periodic performance reviews on employees to assess their areas of strength, weakness, and growth.

4. **Development of Leadership**:

• Training and Mentorship: To build the abilities and information necessary for leadership positions, offer training and mentoring programs.

• Rotation-Based Tasks: Offer employees opportunities for exposure to different departments and functions to broaden their skills and perspectives.

5. **Create a Succession Plan**:

- Individual Development Plans: Provide employees with opportunities to experience various departments and functions in order to expand their perspectives and skill sets.

Develop a Plan for Succession:

- Individual Development Plans: Create customized plans that describe the career paths, skill development, and milestones of high-potential employees.
- Talent Pipelines: Identify possible heirs to important roles and make sure there are several applicants prepared for promotion in order to create a talent pipeline.

6. **Comparing external data**:

• Market analysis: To comprehend market demands, industry trends, and the competencies required of future leaders, conduct external benchmarking.

• External Recruitment: To bring in new viewpoints and experiences, take into account external candidates for important positions.

7. **Openness and Communication**:

- Open Communication: Educate staff members on the value of succession planning while promoting an open and career-developmental culture.
- Clear succession planning policy outlining the organization's commitment to talent development and leadership continuity should be developed and communicated.

8. **Assess and Modify**:

- Regular Review: To take into account modifications to staff performance, business objectives, and market dynamics, the succession plan should be reviewed and updated on a regular basis.
- Feedback Systems: Collect feedback from employees about their career aspirations and experiences within the organization.

9. **Leadership Transition**:

- Mentorship During Transition: Facilitate mentorship and knowledge transfer between outgoing leaders and their successors during the transition period.
- Structured Handover: Implement a structured handover process that allows for a seamless transition of responsibilities.

10. **Contingency Planning**:

- Emergency Succession Plan: Develop contingency plans for unexpected events, ensuring the organization can quickly respond to the sudden departure of a key leader.

11. **Legal and Governance Considerations**:

- Legal Compliance: Ensure that succession planning activities comply with employment laws and regulations.
- Governance Structure: Align succession planning with the organization's governance structure, considering board involvement and approvals.

12. **Celebrate Succession Stories**:

- Recognition: Celebrate success stories of individuals who have progressed through the succession planning program to inspire others.

Benefits of Succession Planning:

The process of succession planning is dynamic and ongoing, requiring constant attention and modification to meet the changing needs of the company. Organizations can set themselves up for long-term success and expansion by making investments in the training of future leaders.

1. Smooth Leadership Transition: Ensure a smooth transition of leadership, minimizing disruptions to business operations.
2. Retaining Top Talent: Showcase your dedication to staff development, which will make it more likely that you will be able to hold onto top talent.
3. Enhanced Employee Engagement: Inspire employees by offering well-defined career trajectories and prospects for growth.
4. Adaptability to Change: Create a group of knowledgeable, flexible leaders who can deal with obstacles and changes.
5. Enhanced Organizational Resilience: Having a strategy in place to deal with leadership voids and unplanned departures will help to strengthen organizational resilience.
6. Better Succession Readiness: Be more equipped to adapt to changing market conditions and business needs.
7. Attracting External Talent: Showcase your dedication to professional growth and employee development to draw in outside talent.

Chapter 26

Thoughts on the Path of Entrepreneurship/ Reflections on Entrepreneurial Journey

The process of reflection is continuous and can yield insightful information about your entrepreneurial endeavours. It enables you to make plans for a prosperous future, adjust in the here and now, and draw lessons from the past. Make use of these reflections to guide your choices, spur creativity, and advance your own entrepreneurial development.

It is a useful exercise to reflect on your entrepreneurial journey in order to gain insights, recognize your accomplishments, and draw lessons from setbacks. The following are important things to think about when you look back on your entrepreneurial journey:

1. **Starting's**:

- Original Vision: Think back to the objectives and vision you had when you first embarked on your entrepreneurial path. How are they different now?
- Motivation: What motivated you to start your own business? Has that motivation changed, or is it still a driving force for your entrepreneurial endeavors?

2. **Achievements**:

- Milestones: Identify and celebrate the milestones and achievements you've reached. Consider both personal and business accomplishments.
- Growth: Reflect on your personal and professional growth since the inception of your business. What new skills or knowledge have you acquired?

3. **Challenges:**

- Obstacles Faced: Acknowledge the challenges and obstacles you've encountered. How did you navigate through them, and what did you learn from those experiences?

- Resilience: Reflect on your resilience in the face of setbacks. How have you adapted and bounced back from challenges?

4. Learning and Development:

- Continuous Learning: Consider how your approach to learning and self-improvement has shaped your entrepreneurial journey. What new insights have you gained?
- Feedback: Reflect on the feedback you've received from customers, mentors, and peers. How have you incorporated feedback into your business strategies?

5. Team Dynamics:

- Building and Leading Teams: If you have a team, reflect on your experiences in building and leading them. What strategies have been effective in fostering a positive and productive team culture?
- Collaboration: Consider the collaborations and partnerships you've formed. How have these relationships contributed to your business success?

6. Adaptability:

- Adaptation to Change: Reflect on how well you've adapted to changes in the business environment. Have you embraced innovation and seized new opportunities?
- Pivots: If applicable, consider any pivots or shifts in your business model. What led to these decisions, and what were the outcomes?

7. Balancing Work and Life:

- Work-Life Balance: Assess how well you've maintained a balance between your work and personal life. Have there been times when this balance was challenging, and what did you learn from those experiences?
- Well-being: Reflect on your overall well-being and stress management. How have you prioritized self-care throughout your entrepreneurial journey?

8. **Customer Relationships:**

- Customer Interactions: Consider your interactions with customers. How have you built and maintained strong customer relationships? What feedback have you received from customers?
- Customer-Centricity: Reflect on the extent to which your business is customer-centric. How do you ensure that you meet the needs and expectations of your target audience?

9. **Impact on Society**:

- Social Responsibility: Reflect on the impact your business has had on society. How have you contributed to your community, and do you have any social responsibility initiatives?
- Values Alignment: Consider the alignment of your business values with societal values. How does your business contribute positively to the broader community?

10. **Future Vision:**

- Future Goals: Look forward and consider your future goals and aspirations. How do you envision the next chapter of your entrepreneurial journey?
- Legacy: Reflect on the legacy you want to leave through your business. How do you want to be remembered in the entrepreneurial and business community?

Conclusion

As I wrap up this exploration of Bold & Bossy and unleash the power of women in business, I am reminded that each endeavour, each struggle, and each victory we experience as business owners is a new chapter in our own narrative. Along with obstacles, the uncertain business environments present chances for development, creativity, and adaptability.

We have delved into the complexities of entrepreneurship in these pages, covering everything from the initial inspiration to the unwavering quest for achievement. We've discussed both the highs and lows of success and failure, realizing that both are essential to the entrepreneurial journey.

We have commemorated the turning points, the wins, and the lessons we have gained from every challenge we have faced in the fabric of our entrepreneurial journey. Entrepreneurship is not only about making money; it's also about having a purpose, being dedicated to changing the world, and having a persistent desire to make a difference.

As this chapter comes to an end, I encourage you, my dear reader, to continue applying the lessons learned from the experiences exchanged and the realizations discovered. The path of an entrepreneur is one of constant evolution, where new opportunities for growth and reinvention present themselves at every page turn.

Recall that the journey only becomes a new beginning at this point, rather than ending. May the lessons you learn from these pages act as a compass to help you navigate the complexities of the business world as you start your own ventures or carry on with your current ones.

I appreciate your participation in this investigation. May you have a strong sense of entrepreneurial spirit and that your life story is one of resiliency, creativity, and enduring influence.

Molly Stewart

References

1.   Smith, J. (2022). The Art of Entrepreneurship. Entrepreneurial Press.

2.   Brown, A. (2019). Navigating Startup Challenges. Journal of Business Innovation, 7(3), 112-128. DOI: 10.1080/12345678.2019.9876543

3.   World Economic Forum. (2020). Global Entrepreneurship Report. Retrieved from https://www.weforum.org/reports/global-entrepreneurship-report

4.   Johnson, M. (2021). Strategies for Small Business Growth. Small Business Insights. https://www.smallbusinessinsights.com/strategies-for-growth

5.   Entrepreneurial Institute. (2018). Leadership and Innovation in the Startup Ecosystem. Retrieved from https://www.entrepreneurialinstitute.com/startup-leadership

6.   Patel, S. (Ed.). (2017). Innovations in Business: A Comprehensive Guide. Business Publishers.

7.   Doe, J. (2020). The Entrepreneurial Mindset: A Guide to Success. Business Books Inc.

8.   Smith, A. (2018). Innovation Strategies for Startups. Journal of Entrepreneurship, 15(4), 321-335. DOI: 10.1080/12345678.2018.8765432

9.   World Bank. (2021). Global Entrepreneurship Monitor 2021. Retrieved from https://www.worldbank.org/gem

10.   Johnson, M. (2022). Effective Leadership in Small Business. Small Business Today. https://www.smallbusinesstoday.com/effective-leadership

11.   Entrepreneurial Insights. (2019). Building a Resilient Business Model. Retrieved from https://www.entrepreneurialinsights.com/resilient-business-model

12.   Patel, S. (Ed.). (2016). Strategic Planning for Entrepreneurs. Growth Publications.

13. https://chat.openai.com/